'This is not only a very beautiful book to re~~~ ~~~~ ~~~~~ ~~t one. Tracing the rhythms a~ ~~~~ ~~~~~ observance, it reminds us o~ ~~~~ ~~~~~ beings. I can't recommend it ~

writer, speaker and ~~~~~ **Cathedral**

'This is a book after my own heart. Nicola Slee, a poet herself, invites us to walk into the woods of a deep Sabbath with the poet Wendell Berry, one of whose beautiful Sabbath poems gives pattern and form to Nicola's new book. She writes with a canny, indeed a weary awareness of all the stresses and pressures of modern life, but against these she sets the wisdom of poetry, of the spirit's song, and of the time-tested patterns and priorities of monastic life. This book is a series of invitations to be still, to go deep, and to hear again the songs that renew our life, the hidden heartbeat that sustains us, and if we will let it, brings us refreshment and renewal. Just dipping into this once a week could be the beginning of your Sabbath renewal.'

Malcolm Guite,
priest, poet and singer-songwriter

'Nicola Slee's volume on the Sabbath is a gentle, yet powerful reminder of the need to take time in our often overstuffed lives for contemplation and self-care. Slee's writing is deceptively gentle, like the warmth of the Sabbath itself. I would highly recommend it, not merely as a read, but also for its reflective questions and blank pages, too. I look forward to encouraging my rabbinical students to read it and gain a different perspective on the value of the Sabbath.'

Rabbi Dr Deborah Kahn-Harris,
Principal of Leo Baeck College, London

'Nicola Slee's book is a welcome, timely, reflective, deeply theological meditation on the practice of "not-doing". Counter-culturally, in informing readers of the wisdom contained in Sabbath traditions, the book celebrates the "essential pause" which enables human life to be more fulfilled, and more clearly shaped by God. It is a welcome invitation to us to find "breathing space in our labours".

Professor Clive Marsh,
Vice-President Designate of the Methodist Church

'Nicola Slee's book on Sabbath is timely, necessary and quietly earth-shaking. Using one of Wendell Berry's Sabbath poems as a skeleton, she enfleshes our deep human need for retreat, space, and creativity. What's more, drawing on her own hard-won wisdom and gift for words, she offers ways for us to begin to claim Sabbath as an embodied reality. Both a study in the topography of prayer and desire, and a workbook towards growth in wisdom, I've rarely read a book that has so thoroughly called to account my feeble efforts to resist busyness.'

Revd Canon Rachel Mann,
priest, poet, writer and broadcaster

'In a deeply personal meditation, Nicola Slee challenges our relentless culture's disordered relationship with time. Using the concept and practice of Sabbath rest (interpreted in myriad ways) she explores how restoring a proper balance between engagement and withdrawal can preserve from burnout our health, our relationships and our natural creativity. At the same time, it can refresh our capacity to relish our lives once more, including the work which we have refused to rest from, which has depleted us. Slee's book made me reflect gratefully on what constitutes "Sabbath" in the patterns of my own life, not only within a weekly rhythm but across the decades.'

Janet Morley,
writer, speaker and retreat leader

'Nicola Slee has written a remarkable poetic meditation on making our lives holy through celebrating the Sabbath. So many have lost sight of this invitation. Slee weaves in her own poetry and journals, and with wise, luminous, challenging prose, calls us to celebrate amidst brokenness and human frailty.'

Gavin D'Costa,
Professor of Catholic Theology, University of Bristol

Sabbath

The hidden heartbeat
of our lives

Nicola Slee

DARTON · LONGMAN + TODD

First published in 2019 by
Darton, Longman and Todd Ltd
1 Spencer Court
140 – 142 Wandsworth High Street
London SW18 4JJ

Reprinted 2021, 2024

Thanks are due to Counterpoint for permission to use excerpts from
the work of Wendell Berry: Copyright © 2012 by Wendell Berry, from
New Collected Poems. Reprinted by permission of Counterpoint
Press; Copyright © 1990, 2010 by Wendell Berry, from *What Are
People For?*. Reprinted by permission of Counterpoint Press;
Copyright © 2013 by Wendell Berry, from *This Day: Collected and
New Sabbath Poems*. Reprinted by permission of Counterpoint Press.
Thanks are due to Many Rivers, for permission to quote from David
Whyte's poem 'Millennium'.

ISBN: 978-0-232-53399-6

A catalogue record for this book is available from the British Library

Designed and produced by Judy Linard
Printed and bound in Great Britain by Bell & Bain, Glasgow

For my colleagues at Queen's
and the Faculty of Religion and
Theology, VU Amsterdam
for the brothers at Glasshampton
and the sisters at Malling
with love and gratitude

Contents

Preface

A Sabbatical story

I didn't plan to write a book about Sabbath when I embarked upon a three-month sabbatical in 2014/15. I set out on a two-month trip to the west coast of the US and Canada and thence to New Zealand (the third month came later, at home), trailing a number of writing projects and plans with me, none of which came to fruition (at least, not then). I got through the American Academy of Religion (the world's largest annual gathering of academic theologians and religious studies scholars) and then began a five-day retreat at the Spiritual Ministry Centre in the funky, laid back Ocean Beach district, right on the Atlantic. I began to feel inordinately tired, but that's not unusual on retreat and I'd been working under ridiculous pressure for months in the lead-up to my sabbatical, so I wasn't particularly surprised or concerned. Dressing one morning, I glanced in the mirror and noticed a vivid red rash on my upper left thigh. I thought to myself 'Shingles' but immediately brushed the thought aside. Only a few days later when talking to my spiritual companion at the retreat centre, did I articulate the thought. A visit to the doctor's confirmed the diagnosis. I was prescribed medication and advised to rest. Shortly after, I moved onto Vancouver where I was staying with old friends I hadn't seen for a dozen years or more. I spent virtually the entire ten days in a stupor, sleeping nine, ten, even eleven hours a night and still waking feeling drugged.

I was incapable of doing anything much except wandering around the house in my pyjamas, watching day-time TV (something I never do in the normal course of life) with my friend, Frances, who has advanced Parkinson's Disease and spends most of her life on her bed. Once or twice we went out to a local café, and I managed the one gig I'd signed up to do at Vancouver Cathedral (thankfully towards the end of my time), but otherwise I saw virtually nothing of Vancouver – except for stunning views as I flew into, and out of, the city.

I was not in any real pain. The rash caused minor irritation, but the main symptom was extreme fatigue, at a level that took me back to my experience of Chronic Fatigue Syndrome some decades earlier. As with CFS, so now, the horizon of my life closed down to the immediacy of my body's needs: the next meal, shower, TV programme and, above all, the next sleep. My brain shut down more or less completely. I couldn't read anything intellectually challenging or emotionally demanding, had no desire to write in my journal, couldn't face the thought of going out anywhere or meeting people, and couldn't even begin to think about any of the writing projects I'd brought with me.

I could have regarded this as a disaster or, at the very least, an irritating intrusion into my sabbatical. Through no great will of my own, I simply acceded to the inevitable and accepted it (I didn't have the energy to fight, and knew that would have done no good anyway). Strangely, there was a gift in being ill (but not so ill that I was in real pain or felt anxious about being away from home). I was compelled to slow down utterly, to abandon all my best-laid plans, and to rest. And then rest some more. If I'd been at home, surrounded by my books and files and constant reminders of the writing projects I'd committed to, I might well have found it difficult to put work down. Being, first, in a retreat centre and then in a family home organized around my friend's chronic illness, gave me permission to let go and give in to the exhaustion without guilt or anxiety. There was something very lovely about spending time with Frances at home, lolling around in our pjs watching TV, making muffins, dancing round the kitchen to one of Frances' favourite CDs, reminiscing about old times. There was a companionable intimacy, a physical and psychological closeness that might have been much more difficult to touch if I'd been well and feeling I should be getting on with my work or impatient to be out and about in Vancouver. For the duration of my visit, we were pretty much on a level; both ill, both tired, both needing rest and care, both content simply to be with each other. It was a beautiful time, and I am immensely grateful for it.

By the time I came to move on to New Zealand, I was beginning to recover. I was met in Auckland by John and Margaret Fairbrother, who welcomed me back to Vaughan Park Retreat Centre (where I had spent a three-month sabbatical in 2009) as if I were family. I was back at the Centre, right on the beach at Long Bay, for a scholars' gathering, which brought together a dozen of the scholars generously funded by Vaughan Park for one or three month scholarships over the previous ten years. Drawn from different continents, we had nothing in common other than the experience of having been at Vaughan Park and loving it enough to want to return for this event. We were women and men, lay and ordained, representing a variety of interests, experience, faith orientations, academic subjects and personalities. Each of us had been invited to offer a presentation to the gathering that might generate good conversation and learning. Typically, John Fairbrother set no stipulations of what form the presentation could take or what the subject matter might be. This resulted in a wonderfully eclectic array of offerings, from readings of poems to academic papers, a singing workshop, an exploration of visual art and a proposal for reforming the United Nations Security Council.

I had been pondering what I could offer in my hour slot. I had a couple of papers I could rehearse, plenty of poems I could read, various topics that could lead to interesting conversation. But none of these seemed to present themselves as the best use of my time, the offering I most wanted to make. The idea began to formulate in my mind of sharing some reflections on the meaning and significance of sabbatical time and space with this group of fellow sojourners, all of whom had experienced sabbatical at Vaughan Park. I felt it could be a rich opportunity to reflect on our different experiences of sabbatical and what our time at Vaughan Park had given us. I hoped that the reflection on Sabbath time and space, whilst focusing on the particularity of our times at Vaughan Park, would have a wider relevance to the keeping of perspective, balance and order in our working lives, beyond the limited sabbatical period. I went back to a much-loved poem by Wendell Berry, the first in his long sequence of Sabbath poems, which I have used on several occasions at the beginning of retreats or quiet days. The poem offered a number of themes and images which would give shape to my thoughts. Having been able to write nothing in the previous four or five weeks, I found my creative energy returning as I worked on my presentation, rooted in Berry's poem and my own experience of the gift of sabbatical time at Vaughan Park. I shared the paper, and it seemed to generate good conversation and resonate with others' experience.

And that might very well have been the end of that. Yet as I returned to the UK at the end of January 2015 and re-immersed myself in work and life back home, the sabbatical theme wouldn't go away. It was something that continued to absorb my attention and energy. It wasn't simply that my sabbatical wasn't strictly over – I had another six weeks to come, having planned to take my three months in two separate stints. It was, I think, a way for me to work on an urgent question that had arisen as a result of having recently gone up from a half-time to a full-time role at Queen's (something I said I would never do, because I had seen the demands made of my full-time colleagues and because I wanted to keep quality time for writing). The question was, how was I going to manage to work full-time in an intense and demanding work environment without making myself ill or endlessly exhausted and without sacrificing the creative inner life represented by my writing, and particularly by poetry? Or to put this another way, how was I going to exercise my new role as Director of Research in a way that modeled the kind of spaciousness and leisure to read, write and do research that I saw (and still see) as central to the role?

Who and what this book is for

So I have written this book, enlarging and expanding the original Sabbatical paper. First and foremost, I have written it for myself, as I suppose most writers do (just as most preachers preach what it is they most need to hear, and hope that others listening in may also take something from their words). I have written it as a way of wrestling with an urgent question about the shape my life needs to assume since the pattern and demands of work have been drastically reconfigured and I have much less time I can call my own for writing and reflection. I want to be intentional about this phase of my life and to shape and craft it as faithfully and artfully as I can.

The decision to go full-time, whilst going against my long-held vow that I would never work more than half-time at Queen's (never say never!), was not one I made lightly, but seemed to be the response that was needed to enable the institution to move forward into a new era. I realized I was ready for the challenge of going full-time and taking up a leadership role within the institution. I had no illusions about how difficult I would find this, and knew that there would be a cost in terms of the amount of time I would be able to protect for my writing. I had fairly recently had a lovely garden room built at home – a place of stillness and reflection, without phone, internet connection or radio – and it was clear I'd get to spend a lot less time in it than I had hoped, over the coming years. Having made the choice knowingly and whole-heartedly to move into this full-time post, I knew I needed to find a way to knit together work and life in a new configuration, in a form that would fit the new demands.

My exploration of Sabbath, then, is a way to find resources for this task of knitting together work and life into an organic whole: a way of working towards a pattern that will hold, that will bind together work, play, prayer and rest in some kind of intentional whole. I want to find a form for the configuration of life and work that is good, healthy, even beautiful, a shape fit for purpose. I want to be able to balance the demands of my role as Director of Research with my own scholarship and writing which I see as central to the work, a necessary part of what I am being asked to do by the institution. Yet, as many scholars in academia bemoan, the very institution that requires us to be research-active frequently loads us with heavy burdens of administration, teaching and management that crowd out significant time to do research. I'm by no means alone in the tensions I experience in my working life and, compared to many of my colleagues at Queen's who bear far heavier loads than I do, I have a great deal of freedom about how I manage my time and considerably more time than they do for research.

And so I did not write this book only for myself. I wrote it for my colleagues at Queen's, as well as for our students, and for other colleagues and friends I know who wrestle with the same questions about how to order the demands of work within a whole that testifies to our deepest values and ideals about God, creation, human vocation and the mission and ministry of the Church. I look around me at my own place of work, but also more widely to university settings where other academic colleagues work and to church and ministry settings, both here in the UK and across the globe. I see colleagues caught in exactly the same dilemmas as me, living out the tension of trying to respond faithfully to too much that is expected of them, with insufficient time and resources, and never being able to catch up with the task, let alone complete it. My colleagues at Queen's are good people, with high ideals and a strong sense of vocation, who give themselves generously to the work to which they are called. They believe in what they are doing, in their capacity to make a difference in the lives of our students and to contribute to a reshaping of the Church's mission and ministry as well as to the broader political culture of our nation and the global community that makes up the wider church and world. All of them, in different ways, bring extraordinary gifts and wisdom to the mission and ministry of the Church. They are people who don't easily withhold from the demands of the institution for which they work; they have an ethic of service, rather than self-gain, which is rare in public life but may still be found, not only in faith communities, but also in the public and voluntary sectors. Nobody goes into any of these spheres for financial gain – though it would be naïve not to acknowledge that there are hierarchies, systems of patronage and privilege, within the Church as much as elsewhere, that still encourage ambition and promote self-interest.

The dilemmas we face are not simply personal ones, of course. Whilst it may be true that every culture and time has experienced the tension between the demands of work and the need for rest and play, this tension takes on a particular character and texture in late postmodernity, in both church and wider society in the Western world (and possibly in parts of the developing world too, although I do not have the experience or authority to speak about these contexts). In a climate of church decline, economic austerity and the 'rationalization' (i.e. drastic reduction) of theological education, fewer and fewer centres of theological learning are required to do more and more, fewer and fewer individuals are required to carry heavier and heavier loads. Year on year since I've been at Queen's (and I've been here over twenty years), I've seen the work demands increase, not only on individuals but on the institution *qua* institution. The structures and systems under which we must operate seem to become ever more complex and demanding. The levels of bureaucracy seem to multiply endlessly. I have heard friends and colleagues in other institutions say the same thing and, now that I am part of the Faculty of Religion and Theology at the Vrije Universiteit, Amsterdam, I see my colleagues there living and working under similarly increasing demands.

So I'm writing this book as much for my colleagues and students as for myself, both at Queen's and in Amsterdam, and for all those myriad others in the church and other professions who seek to live and work according to some moral if not religious compass within compulsive and coercive work cultures that threaten to overwhelm them and suck the lifeblood out of them. I am thinking of colleagues in university departments of Theology no less than other disciplines, those in the Health and Social Services, teachers in primary and secondary education, indeed those who work in just about any professional setting I know – except perhaps those wealthy enough to be able to afford more spacious and kinder working conditions, and to call the shots and charge what they like for their services.

I'm also writing this book for fellow poets and artists who seek to cherish and nurture their vocation to create and yet also have to earn enough to live on. I'm writing it, too, for monastics and all who seek to live their lives as contemplatives in a world that eschews silence, solitude and simplicity. Poets and artists, monks and nuns, are not immune from the tensions and struggles the rest of us face. Indeed, in some ways, they may experience them in a more acute form as those whose vocation puts them at odds with a materialistic and consumerist society (of which I shall say more in chapter 1). Poets, artists and monastics are people I look to for sanity in an insane world, for a sense of what really matters in life. Along with hundreds of others, I go regularly to a monastery – two, actually (Malling Abbey and Glasshampton monastery). I owe much of my sense of faith and the sustenance of my own writing life to these places dedicated to prayer and a rhythm of life attuned to nature and to the needs of the body for rest, manual labour, study and contemplation. And I read poetry more or less every day of my life, and go to hear poets read their work as frequently as I can, for many of the same reasons: to plunge into language sparingly and deeply employed, to seek the wisdom of those who have committed to live as truthfully as they know how, to learn the discipline and the craft of my own art.

Yet poets and monastics feel the strain too. Simon Armitage, in an interview in the Guardian in 2015, spoke of the challenge of building thinking time into a day, and the vital necessity of time for musing, 'doing nothing', in the creative life of the mind.[1] I have written much of this book at Glasshampton monastery, where I often go, and know from my conversations with the brothers here – as well as the sisters at Malling – how hard they work to maintain the profound quality of peace and spaciousness that is evident to anyone who comes here. The work is endless, the monastic community small and many of the brothers elderly: they easily get tired and worn down by their efforts to preserve the rhythm and quality of life to which they are committed

[1] Simon Armitage, 'Making poetry pay', *The Guardian* 26 May 2015: 21-5.

and for which their many visitors hunger. Once a year, I bring a small group of research students to the monastery to housesit for the brothers while they are away on their annual chapter; and this has given me a tiny inkling of the hard work required to keep a large house and garden ticking over, to maintain the daily offices and keep the discipline of silent prayer that is a hallmark of the monastic life.

So I want to offer this book to the brothers at Glasshampton and the sisters at Malling, as well as to my colleagues and students at Queen's, and my newer colleagues at VU Amsterdam, from whom I have learnt and imbibed so much. I have written it, more widely, for anyone who is seeking to build a life that is faithful to the myriad callings of work, home-making, study, creativity, rest, sleep and play, and to forge them all into an organic form, a shape that will hold.

The shape of the book

As I explain in chapter 1, this book follows closely one of Wendell Berry's many Sabbath poems, the first in his long oeuvre of Sabbath poems written over decades.[2] After a general introduction to Berry's Sabbaths project in chapter 1, and a consideration of the nature of Sabbath and how it may function as both resistance and alternative to our harried, hurried culture, subsequent chapters follow the shape of this poem and explore its key themes and images. The poem is repeated at the beginning of each chapter, in order to make reference back to the poem easier for the reader. Each time the poem is repeated, a particular phrase, stanza or section is highlighted in bold, to indicate the main focus of the commentary that follows.

[2] Sabbaths I, 1979, *This Day: Collected & New Sabbath Poems* (Berkeley, CA: Counterpoint, 2013): 7.

In chapter 2, I focus on 'the invitation into the woods' which lies at the heart of Berry's poem and is core to his whole Sabbaths project. The woods represent for Berry the original wilds: the free, uncultivated natural order which is the origin and source of human culture. His poems envisage a constant passage between the woods and the fields, the latter representing land which is cultivated, tended and ordered by human beings but which, without constant labour, reverts to forest. The invitation into the woods is a metaphor, for Berry, of the invitation of Sabbath to come apart from the place of human enterprise, commerce and labour, and to rest in the world-originating beauty of the forest. Of course, the metaphor of going into the woods is an archetypal one, found in myths and fairy stories across the globe and throughout history. Chapter 2 explores the metaphor of the woods, unpacking its range of associations and meanings, and reflecting on the necessary connection between 'woods' and 'fields': between Sabbath time and space and the everyday, six-days world of work and engagement.

Chapter 3 explores 'the invitation to cessation' which is required by Sabbath, the necessary putting-down of our labour and the not-doing which replaces the doing of everyday life, symbolized by silence, rest and the gaps in between any creative human endeavour. Sabbath, I suggest, is the breathing space in our labours, the pause in and before and after the music, the clearing in the woods through which the light comes, the empty dark hours of night in which our minds and bodies regenerate themselves and God gives gifts, treasures of darkness, to God's beloved. Sabbath is, as my title has it, 'the hidden heartbeat of our lives'. 'Heartbeat' suggests the steady, regular rhythm of the heart which animates the human frame, and without which the organism perishes and dies. Yet Sabbath is a largely hidden undercurrent to our lives, part of its warp and weft. The title is redolent of that phrase in Colossians where Paul speaks of the Christian life 'hidden with Christ in God' (Colossians 3:3). Not all that orders and regulates our lives is visible; the grounding of our lives in prayer, sleep and Sabbath rest is hidden from view but absolutely vital, just as the not-doing of Sabbath may look like nothing but is, in fact, the core of it.

Chapter 4 goes on to suggest that, whilst Sabbath may or may not be solitary (it usually is in Berry's 'Sabbath' poems, although in Jewish tradition, Sabbath is largely understood as a family affair), it is always conversational. At the heart of the Sabbath call is 'the invitation to encounter'. This includes conversation with the self and its longings, conversation with others, both near and far, and conversation with God, the source of all life and rest. Sabbath includes the gathering of kith and kin for relaxation, food and refreshment, but it is also a space that is open to the stranger. The Sabbath encounter allows us to engage with the surprising, unexpected parts of ourselves, as well as others who have unexpected gifts to offer.

Two of the four stanzas in Berry's 1979 Sabbath poem concern a mysterious encounter with something or someone fearful, and this forms the substance of chapter 5: 'the invitation to fear'. When we put down our tasks, lay aside our professional roles and identities and enter into the dark woods, who knows what we will find and whether we will ever come out again in one piece? If we dare to take the risk of entering Sabbath space, Berry's poem suggests that we will indeed be confronted by fears, but that these very fears are, at the same time, gifts. As we face the fear of the other, the stranger, the rejected parts of ourselves and the wounded ones we do not want to recognize, gradually the fear leaves us and we hear the music of a song which, we come to recognize, is the gift of our own unique song, our own calling.

Chapter 6, then, goes on to probe this metaphor of the hearing of our own song, 'the recovery of vocation'. At heart, Berry's poem is a poem about recovery, remembering, restoration and transformation. The weary speaker who comes into the clearing in the woods has forgotten who he is, has lost his voice and his song – his vocation and his very identity – through the monotonous stresses and strains of everyday work. We need Sabbath to step back from the habitual round of absorbing activity in order to bring us back to our senses, to enable us to recover our sense of ourselves: to hear our song and to sing it. Sabbath reminds us that we are made for joy, for beauty, for glory: to shine out with the particular glory that is ours and ours alone and that will reflect, in a way that no other life can, something of the glory of God.

Although the woods are deeply restorative, we cannot remain there. Berry speaks of the tension in which most of us live out our lives most of the time, between the solitude and renewal of the woods and the engagement with others and our work in the field. Chapter 7 explores 'the return to the daily', the need to leave the Sabbath space and to re-enter our worlds of work, home and engagement. Berry's poem ends on an apparently unspectacular, utterly ordinary note: 'the day turns, the trees move'. We come back to ordinariness, to dailiness, to the rhythm of things; but we do not return to the six-days world the same as when we left it. Healed by our Sabbath rest, we return renewed and refreshed, reminded of who we are and of our vocation to sing our own unique song and thus to contribute to the world's music. We are content to be part of the wonderful diversity of creatures that make up the world, to play our part in caring for the other creatures, and to lift up our voice to join in the many-splendoured canticle of creation, giving glory and praise to God. So we return again to our labour, until the weekly cycle brings us round once more to the first, primal day of Sabbath when, once again, we put down tools and respond to the call into the woods. So our whole lives are embedded in the rhythm of Sabbath which is God's good and gracious gift to creation.

Each chapter unfolds in a similar pattern. First, the

central idea or theme is introduced and explored by reference to Berry's poem and to his wider Sabbath oeuvre. Then I bring in other references, both from Scripture and from other writers, widening the horizon. I root the discussion in my own life and experience, particularly through the use of extracts from my journals and the inclusion of poems of my own at the end of each chapter. Each chapter also provides questions for reflection and prayer at the end, leading into blank pages so that readers can do their own journaling in response to my own. Whilst designed primarily for individual reflection, this feature of the book could also be adapted for group study and reflection (perhaps particularly in Lent), with group members reading and making notes on each chapter in response to the questions ahead of each meeting.

I have kept a journal throughout my entire adult life, and writing in my journal is one of the main ways in which I endeavour to stand back from my life, see it whole – or at least, see it fresh – and find the form again. Poems, too, are primary forms of meditation, prayerful reflection and artful theology – for me and for many; they are language in compressed form, working intensely to reveal truth beyond and beneath rationality. Much of the thinking, wrestling and praying of the material in this book began life in my journal or my poems, and so it has seemed appropriate to include both journal extracts and poems alongside the main prose content of each chapter. My hope is that the different modes of discourse can speak to each other and unfold something of the many dimensions of Sabbath life and experience.

The journal extracts are not ordered chronologically but chosen to exemplify and embody the themes of each chapter. I have dated them (as unobtrusively as possible, at the end of each extract) for readers for whom it may be helpful to have some sense of their placing in my life. Although I have omitted the odd sentence or two, and sometimes larger sections from these journal extracts where they did not seem relevant, and have occasionally tidied up the spelling and grammar, I have not edited them beyond that.

However it is read and used, I hope this book will support both individuals and groups – whether family, church or other community groups – who are seeking to live more healthy, gentle and disciplined lives within the ecclesia and polis which are constrained by so many pressures. I am very aware that, in many ways, I live a highly privileged life, both materially and in other ways that material security enables. I have the luxury of being able to choose solitude and retreat on a fairly regular basis, in ways that others, particularly those (and they are often women) who care for children or dependent partners or parents, cannot do – or can only do rarely and with much forethought and planning. My ways of thinking about, and practising, Sabbath will be very different from those available to others. Nevertheless, my hope is that my own privileged access to silence and withdrawal can be a resource for others through the pages of this book. If this book encourages others to think more intentionally and critically about the rhythms, patterns and forms of their own working lives – however different from my own – and to seek to practise Sabbath as a form of resistance and an alternative to the destructive, life-denying forces of the market and the machine that invade and dominate public and private life, including the life of the Church, I will be glad. Let the festival of freedom begin![3]

Acknowledgements

Those for whom I have written this book are also those to whom I owe a debt of gratitude. My colleagues and students

[3] Walter Brueggemann describes Sabbath as a 'festival of freedom', in *Sabbath as Resistance: Saying No to the Culture of Now* (Louisville: Westminster Knox, 2014): 43.

at Queen's, over more than twenty years, are some of the best people in the world one could hope to work with, and I know myself to be deeply blessed to be part of such a community, which seeks to model open and inclusive hospitality and to honour the gifts of all within an economy of grace.

As I've said, much of this book was written at Glasshampton monastery, a place I have come to love deeply over the past twenty-five or so years since I have been going there. I am deeply grateful for the gift of this place, on the edge of Shrawley woods where, along with others, I come to soak myself in silence and join the brothers' life of work and prayer for a time. In a different way from Queen's, yet equally powerfully, Glasshampton is a place of generous and open hospitality, a place where the rhythm between the fields and the woods is played out daily in the landscape and the lives of brothers and guests. And although I have gone there rather less frequently since moving to Birmingham, Malling Abbey continues to be a place of renewal and retreat, and I owe the sisters a debt of gratitude for their faithful love and hospitality over more than thirty years. I am conscious of the twin strands of Franciscan and Benedictine spirituality weaving their ways through my life and shaping my Christian practice over many years. The creation-centred, free spirited, questing Franciscan charism is balanced by the stability, conversion of life and contemplative commitment of the enclosed Benedictine life. I love and need them both, and both strands have contributed to my developing theology of Sabbath.

Besides these communities, particular individuals have contributed to this book in ways they may or may not recognize. Frances and Richard Young first introduced me to the poetry of Wendell Berry many years ago when they gave me a slim volume of his 'Sabbath' poems, a gift only exceeded by the gift of their faithful friendship over decades now, since we first met in Cambridge in the early 1980s. John and Margaret Fairbrother, more recent friends, welcomed me to Vaughan Park Retreat on the outskirts of Auckland, for three months in 2009 and then again for the Scholars' gathering in January 2015 which was the occasion that generated the impetus for this book. They are people who embody the free, spacious hospitality of the gospel, that welcomes strangers in, sets a table before them and invites them into conversation and conviviality. Without that gracious hospitality and their friendship, this book would not have come into being.

Donald Eadie, who has accompanied me for many years as a spiritual companion, shows how it is possible to live within the constraints of physical pain and limitation with great trust and receptivity to the life of the world. His small room, where he sits with all sorts and conditions of people, as well as spending many solitary hours of the day and night, has become for me a safe, bounded space where I may yet experience the boundless grace and compassion of God, mediated by a compassionate human other. Donald lives out Sabbath restraint and respect in ways which give me hope for my own advancing years. Within my primary place of work, the Queen's Foundation, David Hewlett continues to offer me regular and supportive space to reflect on the changing shape of my working life and to encourage me to resist taking on more than I can realistically manage. That I often fail to do so reflects my own struggle to live what I write, rather than any lack in his wisdom.

Particular groups have given me the opportunity to try out versions of the material in the book. I am grateful to participants of a Methodist probationers' retreat at The Bield, Ilkley in January 2016 and ordinands from the Lindisfarne Regional Training Partnership on their annual retreat in January 2017, for listening and responding to early versions of chapters in this book, and for praying with me some of the material that follows. They helped me to have faith that the ideas and themes in this book could be of value to others.

A number of individuals have read the manuscript and offered comment and feedback. More than that, they have each taught me, by the ways in which they inhabit their own work and faith, something profound about Sabbath. That David Warbrick, parish priest of All Saints, Kings Heath, Birmingham, not only found time during perhaps the busiest month of a parish priest's year (December) to read the manuscript, but also to give it his searching and unhurried attention, speaks volumes about the kind of priest and person he is. David exemplifies a priesthood that is generous, humane and hospitable, resourced by serious study as well as astonishingly good cooking. David lives out the kind of commitment to Sabbath that I mostly only manage to write about.

Early on in his time at Queen's, my colleague Jonathan Dean and I discovered our mutual love of the poetry of Wendell Berry, and that shared pleasure cemented our friendship. Jonathan is someone whose range of responsibilities and workload have quickly grown far beyond what any one person should, by rights, have to do. Yet his door is almost always open, he manages to look up and smile whenever someone approaches, and he generally gives the impression of having all the time in the world for just that particular person and their precise need, at that precise moment. I hope I might cultivate a measure of his gentle graciousness if I start practising now.

My editor at DLT, David Moloney, warmly affirmed the project from the start, gave me incisive feedback on the manuscript and has shepherded the book through the various stages of production with just the right balance of directiveness and responsiveness. Others at DLT have brought their many skills to the cover design, to processes of copy editing, to marketing and so on. My thanks to Helen Porter, Will Parkes and Judy Linard. I am also grateful to all those who have generously provided commendations of the book, many of whom are good friends and colleagues: Gavin D'Costa, Paula Gooder, Malcolm Guite, Deborah Kahn-Harris, Rachel Mann, Clive Marsh and Janet Morley.

Whilst I have been working on this book, my partner, Rosie Miles, has been living through the painful process of taking voluntary redundancy from her academic post at the University of Wolverhampton, where she has worked for twenty years. Her courage in leaving a job that had, over time, become less and less life-giving, in order to follow her vocation to be a writer and a teacher, is matched only by her determination to find – or perhaps make – a new path. There has been something both ironic and deeply challenging that, just at a time when my own working life has never been more satisfying or demanding, Rosie has faced the death and loss of her own professional role (at least, in its institutional form). For much of the past year or so, we have found ourselves in very different places, requiring us both to dig deep and to ask searching questions about our commitment to work, to a life well lived, and to each other. As a poet, Rosie is deeply concerned with the quest to find the right form, for words as well as for her own life, and she has helped me find the form for many of my poems, both inside and outside this book, as well as continuing to work with me to find a form that will hold our life together. For both, I am more grateful than I can say.

As we have continued to wrestle with what it means to discern and support our different, as well as our common, vocations to life, love, faith and art, our two cats, Tinker and Pumpkin, demonstrate the tactile, animal commitment to Sabbath rest and play in a way that invites us into the same. Their presences weave their way through our lives, and occasionally turn up in the pages of this book – quite properly, as anyone who lives with animals will recognize.

Chapter I

Sabbaths

Introduction

Sabbath is a school for our desires, an exposé and critique of the false desires that focus on idolatry and greed that have immense power for us. When we do not pause for Sabbath, these false desires take power over us. But Sabbath is the chance for self-embrace of our true identity.

Walter Brueggemann[4]

> I go among trees and sit still.
> All my stirring becomes quiet
> around me like circles on water.
> My tasks lie in their places
> where I left them, asleep like cattle.

[4] *Sabbath as Resistance*: 88.

Then what is afraid of me comes
and lives a while in my sight.
What it fears in me leaves me,
and the fear of me leaves it.
It sings, and I hear its song.

Then what I am afraid of comes.
I live for a while in its sight.
What I fear in it leaves it,
and the fear of it leaves me.
It sings, and I hear its song.

After days of labor,
mute in my consternations,
I hear my song at last,
and I sing it. As we sing,
the day turns, the trees move.

Wendell Berry[5]

Wendell Berry and his Sabbath poems

I have long loved this poem, amongst the whole sequence of Sabbath poems that Wendell Berry – farmer, poet, novelist, agrarian activist, cultural critic – has been writing over decades. Born and raised in a farming community in Henry County, Kentucky, Berry gave up a prestigious university career to return to farming in 1965, buying a homestead of his own in order to continue the five-generations long family tradition, where he still lives and writes. In the Introduction to *This Day: Collected and New Sabbath Poems,* Berry describes his Sabbath forays

[5] Sabbaths I, 1979, *This Day:* 7.

into the woods where he walks 'free from the tasks and intentions of [his] workdays' and in which his mind thus 'becomes hospitable to unattended thoughts', 'to what [he is] very willing to call inspiration'. Out of these forays, out of the mind freed from expectations and open to the sights and sounds and life around him, poems may come. Or not. 'If the Muse leaves me alone, I leave her alone. To be quiet, even wordless, in a good place is a better gift than poetry.'[6] The Muse clearly has not left him alone – at least, not for long, and I am among countless readers who must be profoundly grateful for her inspiration. In poem after poem, Berry sounds the depths of the Sabbath theme, writing not only of the human Sabbath in its many aspects and guises, but also of the Sabbath that rightfully belongs to animals, plants and the land, to the planet itself.

This poem, the first of the entire sequence, is one I have often used at the beginning of a retreat or a quiet day, and it is typical of Berry's wider Sabbath project. Luminescent in its simplicity, it yet teases with a mystery that is part of its gift. Deeply earthed in Berry's native land and farming practice, in his long covenant with that land, as well as his Christian faith, I believe this poem possesses a wisdom that can serve as a frame for reflecting on the significance of Sabbath. I want to use it throughout this book as a means of holding and illuminating my own reflections on, and experience of, Sabbath and sabbatical time. It offers a series of metaphors which I shall explore in the coming chapters as ways into a range of themes which I believe lie at the heart of the human, and Christian, journey to find a form that will hold our individual and communal lives with their many complex and varying hungers, needs and desires, and their interlocking patterns of work, rest, play and study, solitude and togetherness. Berry's poem offers a simple but profound

[6] Berry, *This Day*: xxi.

map for my exploration of Sabbath, around which I will weave my own reflections, poems and journal jottings, as well as insights from a variety of other writers – poets, theologians, psychologists, philosophers and naturalists, amongst others.

Berry speaks of 'the idea of Sabbath ... as rich and demanding an idea as any I know'.[7] Like all the great biblical and liturgical rhythms and metaphors, Sabbath is quintessentially simple – one rest day in seven in which to honour God and creation. What could be simpler? A child can grasp it. At the same time, it is an idea of limitless depth, with a spiritual profundity and political bite that are endlessly relevant to any time or place, to all people and cultures. Most particularly, Sabbath is an ideal vital to those harried and oppressed by the relentless rule of the market and the machine, which dictate so much of human life and the life of the planet: regimes dedicated to ceaseless production and consumption, in which rest and genuine creativity play no part. At a time when western governments 'fail to acknowledge that infinite economic growth on a planet with finite resources is non-viable', and 'irresponsibly promote rampant consumerism and free-market fundamentalism',[8] the ideal and practice of Sabbath are more urgent than ever.

The rule of the money god via the market and the machine

As Walter Brueggemann suggests in his little jewel of a book on Sabbath,[9] we in the western world (and increasingly in other parts of the globe too) live in just such a regime. The

---

[7] Berry, *This Day*: xxi.
[8] Open letter by nearly 100 academics to the *Guardian*, 26 October 2018. https://www.theguardian.com/environment/2018/oct/26/facts-about-our-ecological-crisis-are-incontrovertible-we-must-take-action
[9] Brueggemann, *Sabbath as Resistance*.

Church, far from being immune to our production-driven culture, very largely apes and applauds it. Productivity, consumption and the drive to succeed are endemic in church life, potent forces that reinforce rather than challenge the achievement orientation of the world. There is a demand for churches to be 'successful': numerically thriving, financially solvent and able to attract new members. Many such churches promote a brand of Christianity which is juvenile and idolatrous, a 'cheap grace' which promises salvation from all known troubles, success in one's private as well as professional life, security and prosperity in the name of a god who looks and behaves remarkably like the benign patriarch of big business. This is a religion of works and rewards (and therefore, by default, of failure and punishment), a production machine which has nothing to do with the gospel of Jesus.

In a context of church decline and economic squeeze, such as we have been experiencing in the UK for some time now, the Church as well as publically funded institutions such as universities, may be experienced as hard task-masters. If a parish, theological college or university department fails to recruit, increase its numbers and bring in more revenue, it is threatened with closure or amalgamation – and this is no idle threat, as the shrinkage of theological education in the UK over the past twenty years or so demonstrates, mirrored also in the shrinkage of paid leadership roles in most of the churches, and the retraction of departments of theology as well as faculties of arts and humanities in British and European universities.

Yet the rewards of success are, oddly, no less punitive. So in a thriving economy and where church membership is booming, some of the same tensions and dilemmas may be seen. If you do well (whether as a church minister, academic or theological education institution), more and more is expected of you, and there seems to be no limit to the 'more' that can be, or is, demanded. The Church becomes another Pharaoh, anxious about its future and driven by its insecurity to demand more and more from its members and especially its paid representatives: more bricks, more barns, more bums on seats, more innovative mission projects, more training – for less and less. This can manifest as a compulsive, competitive and coercive culture that leaves those who work for it under intolerable pressure, unable to meet the limitless demands, however hard they try. We find ourselves caught in systemic cycles, locked into forms of structural injustice, which operate in spite of the good intentions of individuals, which are self-perpetuating and self-generating. In the end, the system exhausts many who try to live by it (they become disillusioned, give it up, leave), or it breaks them (they become chronically sick or depressed), or it corrupts them (they become little gods in their own religious empires, usurping the worship and the goods that belong, by right, to God alone). In this economy, truth and justice are often sidelined, becoming inconvenient distractions from the ruling law of success. This is what John Hull describes as the rule of the money-god, in which money displaces the rule of God and 'money has literally become the God of our culture'.[10]

In this economy, there is no genuine spiritual depth or creativity. It is a system of surfaces. What matters are appearances, rather than the underlying reality. The successful, confident, ever-upbeat Christian whose gospel is relentlessly positive very often hides a seething underbelly of anxiety, addiction, self-hatred and violence that can never be acknowledged or brought into the light of day. The happy Christian family in which every member is fabulously enterprising and successful frequently masks eating disorders, depression, self-harming, physical or sexual abuse.

[10] John M. Hull, 'Money, modernity and morality: some issues in the Christian education of adults', *Religious Education* 95.1 (2000):12.

The culture of success is so brittle it can never admit of even a momentary slowing of its hectic pace, let alone a genuine cessation. It is endlessly driven, constantly in danger of being judged wanting, of failing to live up to the exacting demands of the Master, whoever the Master may be. Depending on context the Master could be anybody from Bishop to Archdeacon to Vice Chancellor to Prime Minister or President, but these are usually merely figureheads for systems which set the rules and maintain the machines of church and political life. The machine never tires or stops, relentlessly churning out units (whether of hay or money or ball-bearings, ceaseless publications or communications), never needing to pause for rest or food or sleep. The machine simply goes on spewing out its works, greedy to be fed more and more so that it can keep on producing. The more one tries to keep up, respond, feed it, the more the machine demands.

An example: emails and digital communication

A very good example of this, from which virtually no-one in contemporary life is immune, is email, as well as other forms of digital communication and social media. Quick, reliable, cheap and efficient, emails enable immediate communication at the touch of a button around the world. I remember the excitement I felt when I was first able to communicate with friends and colleagues around the world, and how email transformed many routine tasks. Yet who now rejoices in their emails? With the possible exception of my 90-year-old father, who probably gets half a dozen emails a week, none of which is urgent, I don't know a single person who does not experience their emails as a burden. Most of us are checking emails routinely a dozen or more times a day, via mobile phones and tablets as well as laptops and PCs, and many of us carry on doing so long after we have left work into the evenings and even in the middle of the night. The boundlessness of internet communication makes it much harder to set and keep distinct boundaries between the worlds of work and home and, while this flexibility may be advantageous in some respects, it is spiritually and psychologically fraught with danger. Indeed, Archbishop Justin Welby has recently named 'the greatest challenge of the century' as 'how to manage the internet'.[11]

Like all machines, the internet and worldwide web never sleep, generating and proliferating more and more. Although they require human initiative to function, we often feel as if we are in the grip of something with a power beyond us, that we can't control. Rather than reduce chatter and clutter in one's psyche, many of us experience the subtle (or not so subtle) ways in which social media multiply them. Every email responded to almost always generates more, and if one is participating in a group email, it is not unusual for one email to generate a dozen or more replies. The faster one responds to them, the faster the replies come back. The faster we try to placate the machine, the faster it gobbles us up, insisting on more, more, more. So we become slaves to it, devoting every waking moment to its demands – or, even if we aren't actually attending to our emails, the thought of them piling up is somewhere there at the back of our minds. We become addicts to the machine – our mobile phones, laptops, tablets, pcs – and for many of us it has become virtually impossible to switch them off, leave them alone for more than half an hour, let alone half a day.

Of course, machines and markets have their uses, and human life depends on them in many ways. They are not

[11] As reported in 'Welby's "wise men and women"', *Church Times*, 26 October 2018: 4.

adequate, however, and positively harmful, when taken as models for the whole of human living. Berry declares his own antipathy towards machines in a late poem, 'Some further words'. Admitting that he is 'constrained to use them', he nevertheless describes them as 'dire' for the ways in which they use up the world's resources, 'burning' its 'body and its breath'. They are 'neither mortal nor immortal', though they may function as if they will last forever. Berry predicts a time when they will be gone, a day he welcomes as 'a glad and holy day'.[12]

The spiritual dilemma posed by addiction to electrical devices was illustrated vividly in the three-part BBC TV series, *The Big Silence*, which followed five individuals of different ages, backgrounds and beliefs – or lack of them – who signed up for an eight-day silent retreat at St Beuno's, in North Wales.[13] Each of the individuals manifested various resistances to entering fully into the silence, and one young woman in particular, Carrie, had a major struggle to switch off her mobile phone, as the retreat required participants to do (along with not sending emails or otherwise talking to anyone beyond the one hour a day with their allotted spiritual guide). Carrie's mobile phone was her life-line, her connection to the world, her security blanket. By the same token, it was a fetish which kept her from paying full attention to herself and the work of the Spirit in her life. It functioned as a distraction and a protective layer against making herself vulnerable to the silence and to the interior work demanded by the silence. When she finally did manage to switch the phone off and hand it over to her spiritual guide, she experienced a crisis of anxiety and panic, followed

[12] Wendell Berry, 'Some further words', *New Collected Poems* (Berkeley, CA: Counterpoint, 2012): 360.
[13] *The Big Silence*, BBC, 2010, first shown in December 2010. Available at https://gloria.tv/video/HaC3Bg1yPX632WhatEWqEnSZS Accessed 3.1.19

by a significant spiritual breakthrough via a powerful dream which put her in touch with feelings of grief about the loss of her father which she had been avoiding up to that point. She became undefended, able to get in touch with her own raw grief and able to experience the love and presence of God in a way that had been impossible before she handed over the mobile phone.

Recent research in the UK suggests that both children and adults spend vast amounts of time gazing at a screen: up to eight hours a day, which is as much or more than many people work or sleep.[14] This habit of gazing into screens for vast amounts of time each day is having a huge impact, not only on the physical and mental well-being of individuals but also on the nature of culture and social life itself (although there is ongoing debate about the precise nature and extent of this impact). For many people now, reality is quite literally digital. Unless they can record it on their mobile phone and put it up on Facebook for hundreds of others to see, it does not really exist, it is not really happening. *They* do not really exist, *they* are not really 'happening'. The first impulse of many adults and children now, in all kinds of situations from eating a meal

[14] See the 2017 Ofcom report, *Children and Parents: Media Use and Attitudes Report*, for a detailed and nuanced account of TV, online and social media usage in the UK. *https://www.ofcom.org.uk/__data/assets/pdf_file/0020/108182/children-parents-media-use-attitudes-2017.pdf*. Accessed 2.1.19. The research does not speak with one voice, some studies suggesting that large amounts of screen time are detrimental to physical and mental health, whilst other studies argue for no negative side effects. See, for example, https://www.mentalhealth.org.uk/blog/screen-time-and-childrens-mental-health-what-does-evidence-say Accessed 2.1.19. For a review of relevant research literature, see the UNICEF report by Daniel Kardefelt-Winther, 'How does the time children spent using digital technology impact their mental well-being, social relationships and physical activity? An evidence-focused literature review', Innocenti Discussion Paper, 2017-02, https://www.unicef-irc.org/publications/pdf/Children-digital-technology-wellbeing.pdf Accessed 2.1.19.

to witnessing a tragedy, is to record it, rather than simply to experience it or respond to it. What is this doing to our sense of who we are and our capacity for genuine mutual attentiveness, as well as appropriate moral reaction in situations of extremis? When our first instinct is to reach for our mobile phone or camera, rather than to attend to the human person in front of us – either in agony or ecstasy – what has become of human beings? If, in real terms, we devote more time and attention to screens than to the human face, the natural environment, the body of our child or beloved, the work of art in a gallery or which we have purchased to hang on our wall, the religious symbols that dominate the worship space, the architectural space itself with its capacity for evoking transcendence and mystery – what does this say about our real spiritual worship?

Sabbath as a sanitizing temporary reprieve

It is precisely in *this* world of instant and global communication, ceaseless accessibility and availability of information and connection that we need to practise restraint, cessation and Sabbath rest, if we are not to be overcome by the falsification of digital reality. We need, not so much rules, but a rule of life that is wide enough to encompass the new world of social media that is now the norm. Both the principle and the practice of Sabbath have something powerful to speak into our world of ceaseless communication in which reality is constantly created and mediated by the screen. By creating a temporary withdrawal from every form of work and distraction, Sabbath relativizes and destabilizes the all-pervasive, so-called 'reality' of the digital world. The pause of Sabbath, temporary and modest though it is, nevertheless creates a kind of buffer which allows us to step back from the habitual worlds we inhabit and see them for what they are, question them and resist them. We may well go back to these worlds once Sabbath is over – indeed, we have to – but their hold on us has been lessened and loosened. We will switch our mobile phones back on, we will clock into our emails again; but that temporary reprieve enables us to rediscover who and what we are when we are not staring into a screen or tapping messages into a keyboard.

Our own contemporary dilemmas around social media and new forms of technology can seem a world far removed from Wendell Berry's farm and the life he has chosen there. Refusing, as far as possible, modern mechanization, Berry has spent his life farming with horses rather than tractors, and writing with pencil or pen on paper, after which his wife typed up his first drafts on a 1956 Royal standard typewriter. Berry intentionally refused to acquire a computer, let alone any of the other mobile devices I have been commenting on above. In his 1987 essay, 'Why I am not going to buy a computer',[15] he set out his reasons: a commitment to remain as economically and spiritually independent from consumerism and technology as possible; an endeavour to conserve the simplicity of life and the economy of the household in which the tools of his trade are only such as are required and may be purchased and repaired locally, and in which dependence upon a person (his wife) rather than an expensive commodity is an expression of the commitment of their marriage. In a follow-up piece from 1989, 'Feminism, the Body, and the Machine', occasioned by the barrage of critique his first piece had elicited, Berry added another powerful reason for refusing to write with a computer: to resist the mind/body dualism that most forms

[15] Wendell Berry, 'Why I am not going to buy a computer', in *What Are People For?* (Berkeley: Counterpoint, 2010): 170-77. Also widely available online.

of technology promote and to employ the *body* as well as the mind as fully as possible in the creative work of writing (he goes on to give a long, and powerful apology for writing by hand, well worth reading):

> My wish simply is to live my life as fully as I can. In both our work and our leisure, I think, we should be so employed. And in our time this means that we must save ourselves from the products that we are asked to buy in order, ultimately, to replace ourselves.[16]

Berry is now in his eighties, and I have not been able to discover whether he finally succumbed to modern technology and bought himself a computer. Regardless, Berry is a man of his generation for whom the decision not to acquire a computer was a sane and rational one at the time. His reliance on his wife to type up his poems may also be typical of men of his class and generation; most women writers don't have wives who will function as their secretaries! Nevertheless, and notwithstanding such considerations, Berry may be regarded as a prophet whose actions have an emblematic and symbolic significance that goes way beyond his own personal choices. Although I cannot imagine living by his choices, and know hardly anyone who does, I am nevertheless profoundly grateful for the choices he has made (most of them, anyway!), in the same kind of way that I am seriously indebted to those monastics who live out a form of traditional monastic life against the grain of modern life, because they embody a countercultural alternative to the madness that most of us are compelled – or choose – to live.

People like Wendell Berry, and monks and nuns living in

---

[16] Wendell Berry, 'Feminism, the Body, and the Machine', in *What Are People For?*: 190.

monastic communities, create the same kind of boundaries or alternatives in space and time that Sabbath itself, as a practice, creates. These are real spaces, real places, with real people living in them – Berry and his wife in their farm, the brothers at Glasshampton monastery and the sisters at Malling Abbey who have been my friends and companions over many years. However threatened and fragile such places may be (and they often are), simply by being there, they hold out the hope that others, too, may create such alternative spaces and forms of life – likely more compromised, less radical, but nevertheless in the same spirit as that manifested by Berry and the many other advocates of the simple life which have grown up as protests against the monopoly of the machine.

Sabbath, the Temple in time

Sabbath is, for Berry, a discipline lived out within the rhythms of farming, marriage and community life, industry and creative work such as writing. Sabbath is not only for human beings, but also for the land and for all creatures. Sabbath is a profound moral and religious gift, as well as duty; one that contemporary society has largely abandoned but that, if embraced and cherished, has the capacity to renew and heal the fractured and dislocated spirit of present day culture as well as preserve the fragile ecosystem of the earth. In Berry's view, Sabbath demands to be protected and preserved for our sanity and the sanity of the earth and is, at the same time, a way of living that will protect and preserve humanity and the environment, if we learn to live within its gentle, compassionate discipline.

Sabbath is utterly simple and yet capable of endless significance. Chaim Nachman Bialik describes it as 'the most brilliant creation of the Hebrew spirit.[17] Variously described by the rabbis as a bride given by God to her groom, a gift from God's treasury, a Temple in time rather than space, the Chosen Day equivalent to the Chosen People, the Sabbath can be understood as a social, legal, cultural, political and religious institution. Perhaps above all it shapes a particular social morality or theology of *time*. It is both the origin and the apex of the week, a unit of time that seems so utterly 'natural' as to be largely unremarkable, yet is of course a creation, a construction, every bit as much as the synagogue or the church, the Scriptures or the liturgy yet, like each of these, is regarded by Jews and Christians alike as revelation, an illuminating ordinance which offers a glimpse into the nature and ways of God. Christians adopted and transformed Jewish practice of the Sabbath, transferring it to Sunday, the day of Christ's resurrection and thus, for the Church, the first day of the week.

Sabbath is a rhythm within the Jewish and Christian week, most obviously. It may also be applied analogously to smaller or larger units of time. The principle of temporal pauses within a larger unit of time is infinitely flexible. It may be applied to the pattern of the day, the rhythm of the week or to larger units of time such as the three month academic or clerical sabbatical every five or seven years. The monastic offices are an example of the Sabbath rhythm of pausing from labour throughout the day (and night). The biblical injunction to celebrate every seventh year as a Sabbath rest for the land, and every fiftieth year as a Jubilee, represents a larger and more extensive application of Sabbath. Whatever the scale on which Sabbath is imprinted, it is what Judith Shulevitz calls 'God's claim against our time', implying that *all* time 'has an ethical

---

[17] Chaim Nachman Bialik, quoted in Judith Shulevitz, *The Sabbath World: Glimpses of a Different Order of Time* (New York: Random House, 2010): xviii-xix.

dimension'.[18] It makes its ethical and religious claims in an utterly practical way, however, through the ordering and celebration of specific times and seasons. 'The Sabbath is an organizing principle. It is a socially reinforced temporal structure'.[19]

Sabbath as labour and gift, the day of days

Whereas, for Jews, Sabbath is the last day, the climax of creation, for Christians it is the first day of the week, the first day of the rest of our lives. For both Jews and Christians, Sabbath is the primal day, the day of all days, feast of all feasts. It is George Herbert's 'but one day' and that one 'ever'.[20] It is the *only* day we are ever given: *this* day (the title of Berry's collected Sabbath poems). '*This* is the day that the Lord has made', the psalmist declares; 'let us rejoice and be glad in it' (Psalm 118:24).[21] There is only ever *today* in which to hear God's word, be glad and respond. As the writer to the Hebrews admonishes his (or her) hearers: 'But exhort one another every day, as long as it is called 'today', so that none of you may be hardened by the deceitfulness of sin' (Hebrews 3:13). What is 'the deceitfulness of sin' but the delusion that time is our possession and under our control to marshal and use as we will, that every day is like another, that no day or hour belongs to God, that past and future are places where we may live. But Scripture says, 'Today, if you hear [God's] voice, do not harden your hearts as in the

---

[18] Shulevitz, *The Sabbath World*: 24.

[19] Shulevitz, *The Sabbath World*: xxix.

[20] George Hebert, 'Easter', in C. A. Patrides (ed.) *The English Poems of George Herbert* (London: Dent & Sons, 1974): 62.

[21] All biblical quotations are from the New Revised Standard Version, unless otherwise stated.

rebellion' (Hebrews 3:15). Interestingly, Hebrews goes on, from this injunction to be present in the only day we are ever given, to reflect on the Sabbath rest into which we are called. The work of 'today' is, paradoxically, the 'work' of entering into God's promised Sabbath rest:

> So then, a Sabbath rest still remains for the people of God; for those who enter God's rest also cease from their labours as God did from his. Let us therefore make every effort to enter that rest, so that no one may fall through such disobedience as theirs. (Hebrews 4:9-11)

There is great psychological and spiritual perception here, for it is indeed a labour requiring much persistence and resistance to lay down the tasks and demands that endlessly assail us, and enter into that Sabbath rest. The Sabbath is given, it comes round with unfailing regularity, week by week; but it only *becomes* Sabbath as we enter into it, lay aside ordinary time and enter into sacred time, God's boundless playtime, rest time, Eden time. Wendell Berry's poem shares the wisdom of the letter to the Hebrews for it, too, recognizes that Sabbath is a time and space that must be entered intentionally. We must leave the labour of the fields in order to go amongst the trees and sit still.

Journal entries

I realize that the search for a Sabbath rest and rhythm is not a new theme in my life but one that's been around for a long time. I have always been inclined to over-extend myself, to give myself away too deeply and intensely and then to experience an answering depletion, an exhaustion of being that can take days, weeks – and at certain points in my life, months – from which to recover. Leafing through an old journal in search of something else, I came across the following passage:

'You are not a machine', I keep telling Rosie – but I need to heed my own wisdom! I am not a machine. I am a human being. If I am spurned or the offering of my deep places rejected, it hurts. If I am knocked, I bruise, I bleed. If my beloved is hurt and wounded, I hurt, I ache. If I spend myself to the uttermost, I am depleted, I am exhausted. If I constantly demand much of myself, I need also to take care to cherish and nourish myself. If I empty my cup, I need to set it down under the flow of the stream, where it may be replenished. If days are given to the encounter with the other, the pouring out of self to and for the other, there need to be times of withdrawal, where I take myself far away from others in order to rediscover who I am in my solitude. If language forms the medium of my trade and I am immersed in the business of words, I need to plunge deep down beyond the surface of words into the abyss of silence. I need to recover the rhythm and the flow that will uphold my life: spaciousness to counter the fullness, slack

44

times to recover from intensity, aloneness after much encounter, silence after speaking, sleep after a long day's work, walking, swimming or dancing after too much sitting, releasing into the body after long hours inside my head, relaxation after tautness, play after serious work, cuddles after hard knocks, darkness to assuage the light, night to swallow up and repair the ravages of day. I am not a machine. I am a human being, made for the rhythms of creation, in search of a Sabbath rest.

(undated)

It's half-term, I'm at Glasshampton again with a small group of students and colleagues house-sitting for the brothers while they are away on chapter.

Today is my one day when I'm not ferrying or fetching anyone anywhere, when I'm simply here, and no distractions. That is so precious and soon will be gone (we leave tomorrow, though not 'til the end of the day)...

One might think, on a clear day like today, that I'd just want to crack on with work, tackle any one of a dozen or more tasks and projects I brought with me. But I don't. I desperately crave the soul food of silence, prayer. I am parched for the river of God. 'O God, you are my God, I seek you, my soul thirsts for you; my flesh faints for you, as in a dry and weary land where there is no water' (Psalm 63:1).

The silence and the common life of prayer and work, the beautiful surroundings of the monastery, put me in touch with what I most desire: God, and to walk in God's ways. When I'm too busy at home, and the space and prayer get crowded out, pushed to the edges, then I lose the sense of God drawing me, pulling at my heart.

Like breeds like. Silence, meditation, praying, living at a sane, gentle pace breed more of the same: a quiet heart, contented body, a mind set free to reflect and think deeply, piercing beneath the shallows; a soul at peace with itself. God looks upon the mirror of the settled soul and can see her own image reflected there. The soul gazes at God and is one with the beloved.

By contrast, noise, hurry, frenzy, living too much in one's own head, pushing the limits of the day and the night, sitting for too long at a desk without moving; these breed anxiety, discontent, weariness, a mind that can no longer think straight, a harried, impatient spirit and a body utterly out of sorts, manifesting all kinds of pain and discomfort. God seems to retreat and depart the frenzied soul; only because the longing for God and prayer have been squeezed out by so much clutter. The demons of avarice, gluttony, anger, pride – or contemporary forms of them such as drivenness, competitiveness, fearful striving, inability to rest or put one's work down, the irritability and anger borne out of exhaustion and frustration – these all come to take up residence in the soul where God yearns to reside. Never insisting or imposing on the beleaguered soul, God is content to be pushed out of the world, relegated to the margins. At the edges of our lives, consciousness and communities, God waits like a hungry beggar, 'til we notice him there, invite her back in to sit and eat at our soul's table.

So, instead of moving straight to my work, I walk out round the back of the monastery, into the garden scattered with snowdrops, primroses and celandines, the fat, tight buds on the Magnolia tree full of promise. Almost at once, I'm in tears – weeping for the life I do not lead (the one I practise here for a week and then largely abandon), the life I long for, the God I keep at arm's length, the yearning that takes up residence in my heart as soon as I give her any space...

(21.ii.19)

Sabbatical

Live like the rain: taking its time,
in no hurry to stop, drenching
the thirsty ground, simple and serious.

Live like the garden: soaking it up,
taking the goodness deep within,
giving back beauty and green.

Live like the cat: stretched out
under the rosebush, giving herself
to sleep in the delicious morning.

Live like you believe in your life – even
love it: like it's the gift you say it is,
not any kind of punishment

As you go backwards and forwards
up and down the garden path
living the life you are called to love.[22]

---

[22] Nicola Slee, 'Sabbatical', originally published in *Theology* 120:1 (2017): 39 (adapted and revised).

Questions for reflection and prayer

- *What does the notion of Sabbath mean to you or for you?*
- *In what ways, if at all, do you mark Sabbath – as a pause in the week, as pauses in the day, or as pauses in larger units of time (for example, an annual holiday or retreat)?*
- *Do you feel largely positive or negative about the Sabbath command? Or a mixture of both? Has this changed for you over time?*
- *In what ways do you experience 'the rule of the money god'? How do you regard and experience the regime of the market and the machine?*
- *Would you say you were addicted to anything? If so, what form does your addiction take? Substance (alcohol, caffeine and so on)? Particular practices and habits (watching TV, blogging, social media use, etc.)?*
- *How much time do you spend looking at screens? What effects does that have on you and your relationship to self, others and God?*
- *In what ways do you hunger for Sabbath?*

Thoughts
and notes

Chapter 2

I go among trees
The invitation into the woods

One learns more in the woods than in books. The trees and the rocks will teach you things you will not hear elsewhere.
Bernard of Clairvaux[23]

For myself, solitude is rather like a folded-up forest that I carry with me everywhere and unfurl around myself when I have need. I sit at the feet of the great old trees of my childhood. From that vantage point, I ask my questions, receive my answers, then coalesce my woodland back down to the size of a love note til next time.
Clarissa Pinkola Estés[24]

[23] Letter 101 to Henri Murdach, Abbot of Vauclair, quoted in *Cistercian Abbeys: History and Architecture* (Köln: Könemann, 1998): 25.
[24] Clarissa Pinkola Estés, *Women Who Run with the Wolves: Contacting the Power of the Wild Woman* (London: Rider, 1992): 294.

I go among trees

I go among trees and sit still.
All my stirring becomes quiet
around me like circles on water.
My tasks lie in their places
where I left them, asleep like cattle.

Then what is afraid of me comes
and lives a while in my sight.
What it fears in me leaves me,
and the fear of me leaves it.
It sings, and I hear its song.

Then what I am afraid of comes.
I live for a while in its sight.
What I fear in it leaves it,
and the fear of it leaves me.
It sings, and I hear its song.

After days of labor,
mute in my consternations,
I hear my song at last,
and I sing it. As we sing,
the day turns, the trees move.

Wendell Berry[25]

The woods as literal and metaphorical wilds

In poem after poem, Berry writes of the landscape which is his ground, the fields and the woods and the lanes he knows like the back of his hand, that he has helped to shape and nurture, and that have nurtured and shaped him. These are

[25] Sabbaths I, 1979, *This Day*: 7.

not just any trees: these are trees he knows intimately, woods he has walked in countless times, land he has trodden over and over. This is the land he has chosen as the one place to dwell – or that has chosen and called him. At the heart of this poem is an invitation into the woods: an invitation to intimacy and conversation with the natural landscape which is the source and ground of human livelihood and wisdom.

I propose to explore the invitation into the woods at both a literal as well as a metaphorical level. At the literal level, the poem is an invitation into the wild, free spaces of nature that still exist at the edges of human society, though eroded and endangered, and, in microcosm, may still be found within even the most built up urban environments. The woods represent the natural wilderness which Berry knows is essential for human sanity and salvation, and can encompass not only trees and forests but also lake, river, beach, mountain, desert. At a metaphorical level, the poem is an invitation into the wild, free spaces of the psyche: the inner spaces of play, creativity, imagination and dream, the realm of the subconscious and symbolic which is equally essential for human sanity and salvation. Both literal and metaphorical levels are, of course, profoundly inter-related. The preservation and cultivation of natural wilderness spaces are a precondition of human creativity and freedom. We cannot have one without the other. Most human beings recognize this, at an intuitive if not a rational level. Even the most relentlessly urban amongst us recognize the refreshment and rejuvenation to be found by withdrawing from the city into natural spaces, and many of us find such a rhythm of withdrawal essential to our physical and psychological well-being.

Berry certainly knows his dependence on the natural order, an order he respects and seeks to work with and learn from. As Philip H. Pfatteicher argues in his classic work, *Liturgical Spirituality*:

We are not strangers on the earth, nor are we its lords.

We are not independent. We come from nature; we exist by the processes of nature; we live every moment in absolute dependence on nature. We can live some five weeks without food, five days without water, five minutes without air. We cannot be against nature; we can only be one with it. If out of ignorance or apathy or aggressiveness we tear the fabric of which our own life is a part, we destroy ourselves as well as the mighty structure from whose womb we were born, in whose web we have had our unfolding history, and whose support and companionship in life is the primal place and ground of our existence.[26]

Today, as never before, we are aware of our profound dependence on the natural order and of the ways in which we are destroying the very earth which is our home, polluting the seas and rivers which are its and our lifeblood, and poisoning the air we and all creatures need to breathe. The recently published United Nations IPCC report on climate change catalogues the myriad ways in which human consumption, unfettered use of fossil fuels and largescale industry is creating havoc in the warming of global temperatures, the melting of the icecaps and the rising of the seas. Low-lying islands such as those in the Pacific and huge areas of Asia which have seen drastic deforestation and thus have been deprived of protection against flood and tsunami are already bearing the brunt of climate change. Wealthier nations in the northern hemisphere such as the UK and US may feel the effects of global warming less acutely, but most of us recognize the signs of the times in changing patterns of weather, from longer, dryer, hotter summers to more extreme rainfall and storms throughout the cycle of the year. The UN IPCC report warns that we have only twelve years

---

[26] Philip H. Pfatteicher, *Liturgical Spirituality* (Valley Forge, Pennsylvania: Trinity Press International, 1997):106.

to limit climate change catastrophe and to turn back from the brink of irreparable climate change.[27]

Sabbath, as a principle of cessation, restraint and the honouring of the rhythms of the natural world, has much to say to a world on the brink of climate catastrophe. The call of the woods is not least a call to urban humans who have forgotten their roots in nature to leave the bright city lights, if only for a few hours or a few days, and to renew their covenant with the woods, the fields, the rivers and seas, the moors and lakes, at the same time as to immerse in the natural cycles of daylight and darkness, night and day, which are blurred and erased in the city. Such an invitation is not only for rest and relaxation – though it most certainly includes these – but more profoundly for a renewal of our connection to the originating sources of nature and the cyclical rhythms of the seasons.

The natural world with its annual cycles of birth and death, flourishing and waning, harvesting and decay, can teach human beings a respect for similar cycles within our own individual, social and communal lives. In the city which never sleeps – rather like the machine which never stops – we can easily be deluded into supposing that we, too, can live without recourse to rest, sleep and cessation, or at least to recognize our need for these only begrudgingly and when at the edge of our limits. Urban life necessarily privileges light, activity, social intercourse and conviviality, productivity and commerce. The pace of city life tends to be quick and intense, made for the young who are, increasingly, its architects, and predicated on the speed of the car, train and tram. Modern cities, especially in the US, are not made for walkers but for drivers. European cities tend to be on a smaller scale, particularly those that survive from earlier centuries, and their streets are often more convivial to

[27] UN Intergovernmental Panel on Climate Change Report (2018), available at https://www.ipcc.ch/sr15/ Accessed 2.1.19.

someone getting around by foot. Even so, the pace of city life is rarely unhurried. The larger the city, the faster it goes. Capital cities such as London seem to function at a frenetic pace. Everyone is hurrying from street to underground back to street again, from home to work and back again, from one appointment to the next (unless, of course, you are unemployed or homeless with nowhere to go and nothing to do). I am conscious that, when I go to London, I get swept up in this frenetic pace – which is both exhilarating and exhausting (and therein lies some of its compulsive attraction; if it were *only* exhausting, it would be much easier to resist!). I walk faster, think more frenetically, rush headlong into the day, in order to keep up with everyone else. Trying to go slow on an escalator going down to the underground, for example, one is likely to get pushed aside or to fall. It is potentially dangerous to try to buck the trend and stop the flow, easier to offer no resistance and to melt into the fast-paced city thrum.

Withdrawing for a time, however brief, into the wild spaces that still exist, offers a reprieve from this fast-paced, furious urban living. To respond to the invitation into the woods is to offer ourselves an opportunity to gaze on beauty and decay (the two go together, not to be parted), to stretch our cramped and stressed bodies in revivifying exercise, to rest in the deep darkness of the countryside and to see beyond the horizons of a manmade environment into a sky studded with light from planets thousands of light years away. Such stepping aside into the space of 'the woods' not only rests and restores our bodies but renews and revitalizes our minds and reminds us that it is possible to live at a different pace and in touch with wider, more elemental horizons than those by which we are habitually enclosed. Our brains are permitted to slow down and stop, our imaginations are cleansed and renewed. At the same time, our profound connectedness to the natural world and our ethical responsibility to care for it, are re-woken in us. Thus the invitation into the woods is not only an invitation to renew and refresh the jaded human; it is a very real invitation to renew and repair the desperately damaged fabric of the creation itself crying out for healing. To refuse the invitation to honour Sabbath is to refuse our own renewal but also that of the entire created order of which we humans are a small, though potentially catastrophic, part. To put this more positively, the invitation into the woods is an invitation to renew our covenant with ourselves, with the natural world, with our fellow creatures and with God.

The sacred life of trees

The metaphor of going into the woods is an archetypal one, found in myths and tales across the globe. The woods are a magical place of deep and ancient spirituality – a place of primal, pagan encounter with fairies, elves, witches and elemental spirits of the wild. From time immemorial, trees have been held as sacred and worshipped, and continue to be revered by many influenced by paganism as well as Celtic spirituality. Sacred groves and individual sacred trees are places of pilgrimage in rural England, Wales, Scotland and Ireland, as well as further afield. Trees marked out by age, size and rarity may be particular objects of veneration, such as the few remaining Kauri trees of Aotearoa New Zealand, the Redwoods of California and the Indian Banyan. Pilgrims tie ribbons, strands of cloth, flags and prayer beads around the limbs of trees and leave tokens of worship and pictures or photos of people for whom healing or blessing is sought. Myths and stories both ancient and modern reflect this sense of the spiritual power and wisdom of trees. Think Narnia, think Middle Earth, think Babes in the Wood, Hansel and Gretel or Robert Frost's 'Two roads diverged in a yellow wood',[28] itself echoing the beginning of Dante's *Divine Comedy*[29] – the list is potentially endless.

Roger Deakin's *Wildwood: A Journey Through Trees*[30] is a marvelously informative and enchanting exploration of the native woods of Britain, confirming the huge and varied practical usefulness of wood as well as the natural and metaphorical significance of the forest. Deakin regards woods as 'the subconscious of the landscape', 'the guardians of our dreams of wildwood liberty, of our wildwood, feral, childhood selves'. 'They hold the merriness of Merry England, of yew longbows, of Robin Hood and his outlaw band. But they are also repositories of the ancient stories, of the Icelandic myths of Ygdrasil the Tree of Life, Robert Graves's "The Battle of the Trees" and the myths of Sir James Frazer's *Golden Bough*. The enemies of woods are always the enemies of culture and humanity.'[31] Deakins points out that, in many myths and in Shakespeare's plays, people go into the woods (and often get lost along the way) in order to find themselves, to grow, learn and play. Deakin also reminds readers that woods are 'havens for intimacy', for sexual as well as other kinds of fecundity. Walking in woods with Ronald Blythe, Blythe commented how 'all country children ... were conceived in woods, because the cottages were simply too full of other people. Children, grandparents and others lived hugger-mugger in the cramped rooms, so couples adjourned to the woods for privacy'.[32]

In researching the life of trees, scientists, too, contribute enormously to our perception of the hidden wisdom and

[28] Robert Frost, 'The road not taken', at https://www.poetryfoundation.org/poems/44272/the-road-not-taken. Accessed 2.1.19

[29] Dante's *Divine Comedy* begins, 'In the middle of our lives' journey, I found myself in a dark wood'.

[30] Roger Deakin, *Wildwood: A Journey Through Trees* (London: Penguin, 2007).

[31] Deakin, *Wildwood*: xii.

[32] Deakin, *Wildwood*: 44.

sociability of the forest. In the international bestseller, *The Hidden Life of Trees*, for example, Peter Wohlleben provides evidence for the ways in which trees communicate with each other via their roots, warning each other of impending crisis, protecting themselves from attack by releasing chemicals into the air or toxins into their leaves, and many other fascinating facts which are slowly transforming human appreciation for the sophistication and subtlety of arboreal life.[33]

Although Berry's poem doesn't mention it explicitly, the invitation into the woods is surely an invitation to *play* (the poem does mention music, which is perhaps close to play, and music-making is often a feature of the stories and myths about the greenwoods). Sabbath is the invitation into the free, wild space where we may play with the magic of the woods, explore off the beaten path, enter the unbounded space of our hearts and imagination. It's the invitation to pursue the ideas or reading that we didn't plan to do; to think outside the box; to follow leads, hunches or dreams that weren't part of our original sabbatical agenda. It is the entry into the freefall of sabbatical where the normal rules fall away and we enter a time and space more organic, more spontaneous, full of serendipity and unexpected synchronicities.

In Scripture, the creation of humanity is set within a garden of lavish vegetation and trees that are 'pleasant to the sight and good for food' (Genesis 2:9). Two trees of particular symbolic significance – the tree of life and the tree of the knowledge of good and evil (Genesis 2:10) – testify to the deep connection between trees and life, woods and wisdom. Many stories suggest that the spiritual veneration of trees continued in Jewish and early Christian practice, rather than being banished:

---

[33] Peter Wohlleben, *The Hidden Life of Trees* (London: William Collins, 2017).

Adam and Eve tasted the forbidden fruit from the Tree of Knowledge in Paradise; the Lord first appeared to Moses in the vision of a burning thorn; Abraham settled near a sacred grove of turpentine trees, where the Lord appeared to him, and he had a vision while sleeping under an old and venerated oak tree; the prophetess Deborah dwelled under a sacred palm tree when the children of Israel came to her for justice, and was eventually buried beneath the sacred oak of Beth-El. Scriptures from the New Testament related that Jesus taught his disciples in the sacred olive grove of Gethsemane, and retreated to the grove on the last night of his life. In Gaul and other places in Europe, the earliest Christian teachers preached under sacred trees and erected altars and churches beside them.[34]

Throughout the psalms and prophetic books, as well as in the gospels, trees are employed as images of social, spiritual and personal flourishing (e.g. Psalm 1:3; 52:8; 92:12; Proverbs 11:30; Jeremiah 17:8; Matthew 3:10; 12:33). The image of a tree of life which stretches from earth to heaven, connecting humanity and God, is found in many of the world's religions. Because of their immense age, size and capacity to endure, to renew, to bear fruit and supply timber, trees have become symbols of transformation and renewal, but also of stability and faithfulness – trees grow slowly and outlive humans by decades, if not centuries. In Christian theology, the cross has been interpreted since earliest times in terms of the tree of life, the sacrificial outpouring of Christ on the cross undoing and reversing the sin of Adam and Eve who took from the forbidden tree. The Bible ends with a vision of the new Jerusalem in which the tree of life flourishes by the river flowing from the throne of God, bearing leaves 'for the healing of the nations' (Revelation 22:2).

[34] Christine Zucchelli, *Sacred Trees of Ireland* (Cork: Collins Press, 2016): 9.

In the medieval West, according to Jean-Françoise Leroux-Dhuys, the forest came to stand for the desert of the earliest abbas and ammas, and monasteries were always built in or on the edge of the woods:

> Here [the monks] could find the 'solitary wastes' dear to contemplatives, but also the wood that provided the necessary material for the various crafts. The forest-wilderness had preserved its mythical character as the temple of pagan cults and the refuge of runaway serfs, charcoal-burners, hunters of wild honey, and other woodland folk who wandered in the forest like nomads in the desert. They were regarded with suspicion by those of fixed abode, and they endowed the forest with a marginality that had always attracted hermits and was still appealing to the cenobites. [35]

Learning from the wisdom of the woods in my own life

I grew up on the edge of woods and communed with trees every day of my life, as I still do. Our farm lane was lined with trees: little, stunted things that were blown near horizontal by the westerly winds and never grew bigger than the size of a human. It was less than a mile down the lane and through our fields to the old woodland fringing the North Devon coast, where my father and uncle would go to collect holly every winter and where we children would forage and play among oak, ash, beech, rowan, ivy and holly.

I had one particular tree that I looked out for every morning and evening on the school bus (it's still there and I still look out for it when I take the road from Bideford to

[35] Leroux-Dhuys, *Cistercian Abbeys*: 46.

Clovelly). It grows on its own, sticking up out of the hedge and poking its bent branches into the sky, at the top of Fairy Hill (and how appropriate is *that* name?). I loved it, particularly in winter, when its white, skeletal form had an austere beauty that was made all the more striking by the backcloth of the setting sun at the end of the school day. Every day, Monday to Friday, I greeted that tree silently, as surely as I greeted my grandfather every morning when he came into the farm kitchen bringing buckets of milk from the morning's milking.

I also loved walking in the woods in and around Hartland and Clovelly, at first with the family. Mum always led these expeditions into the woods, usually to Mouth Mill via Clovelly Court or Brownsham. The memorial cross to two babes in the wood who had got lost and died made a deep impression on us as children, an overt expression of the underlying sense of threat we felt but did not articulate. There was one oft-recalled occasion when we missed the footpath and got lost, and had to crash our way through dense undergrowth back to our fields. Jane and Peter, who must have been about five or six at the time, tagged along at the end and started wailing, convinced we were going to meet a similar fate to those two children.

Later, I'd go walking the lanes and footpaths on my own. I spent much of my teenage years, when I wasn't at school or in the house, wandering the fields and woods in long, cheesecloth skirts and sandals, carrying my Bible, notebook and a volume of poetry. I read Gerard Manley Hopkins for the first time in lush fields near Abergavenny one summer when I was nannying for a family with two small children. The power of the words, their rhythm and sound, in such a setting, knocked me sideways – even though I didn't understand half of it. I wrote my own, very bad, verse mostly in fields and woods.

I will never forget my first term in Cambridge, walking

along the backs, as the leaves were turning crimson and gold, and then began to fall. I'd never seen such tall, majestic trees before – or, if I had, I hadn't really noticed them. I thought all trees were like the lichened, wind-bent grotesques of my North Devon childhood, and suddenly, here were these soaring, airy creatures stretching up, up, up into the wide Fen skies, going on for ever. I spent that first term with my head in the clouds, almost literally, as I gazed and gazed into the branches of those beautiful, stately elms (sadly felled by Dutch Elm Disease ten years later). It's a wonder I didn't walk into them and knock myself out.

Many years later, when travelling further afield from home, I experienced a still deeper awe and wonder in the presence of even larger and more sublime trees, thousands of years old, such as the Kauri in the North Island of New Zealand, and Californian Redwoods. It had never seemed strange to me that human beings should venerate trees, but these huge totems had a towering presence in the landscape that could only be described as god-like, and I understood in a new way the impulse to worship.

I now live in urban Stirchley, in the middle of Britain's second city, yet we are surrounded by trees on every side. From the street, it's impossible to guess at the world of green out the back. All the gardens on our humble ex-council estate are planted with trees and, though some people have had trees taken down, many survive and new ones are planted. We inherited a Bramley at the bottom of the garden which gives us a crop of fine cooking apples every year; we have added a small eater, rowan and hazel, and taken out two leylandiis from the rockery, enabling the lilacs to fill out into little trees in their own right. Although it's in next door's garden, the tree nearest the house is a delicate silver birch whose leaves are never entirely still and whose branches provide homes to nesting birds. We watch it, day in, day out, from the bedroom window. Further afield there are limes, mock orange, willows, poplars, spruce and May-trees of various ages and sizes dotted around in neighbouring gardens.

Then there is the dense privet hedge on one side of the garden which provides habitat for insects, birds and small creatures. All the houses on the estate would originally have had hedges and, though some survive, many have been uprooted and replaced by fences, which are so much uglier, more precarious (our panels are always being blown out by the wind), less durable and far less hospitable to the flora and fauna and ecology of the landscape than a hedge. We had to argue with our neighbour to keep the hedge, but it's something we feel strongly about and are committed to maintaining. For me, it's also a connection with my Devon childhood, where hedges are a major feature of the landscape. The massive, earthen banks planted with trees and every kind of wild flower line all the lanes and minor roads, enclosing thoroughfares in a dense, shady, secret green world like an underground or underwater realm. In these lanes you can often see very little, just a patch of sky and the odd flash of a field as you pass a gate. They are their own ecosystem of plant and wildlife, a kind of forest growing up the sides of the roads and the tracks, and they help to create the sense of a hidden, secret landscape a world away from the motorways and vast tracts of flat arable land in other parts of England.

I learnt all the wild flowers I know from walking Devon lanes and discovering the flowers in their seasons, picking handfuls of them to bring home (I suppose one wouldn't do that now) and consult my flower book or, more often, my grandmother who knew all their country names. Of course our privet hedge has nothing of this profusion of wild flowers, but it does sprout bramble, ivy, knotweed and even a raspberry plant, and provides shade for snowdrops and bluebells, as well as nesting for the birds.

Before I came to Birmingham, my image of the city was

of a great industrial wasteland, an urban sprawl dominated by concrete motorway networks, high-rise council flats, endless streets and ugly industrial estates. Of course, it has all of that, but I was astounded to discover it is, in fact, one of the greenest cities I've ever visited. John Hull used to say, 'for every person, a tree', and it's true. The southwest of the city is particularly blessed with parks and many of the arterial routes into the city are tree-lined with great green breathing spaces running down their centres. I suspect the Cadburys, in developing this whole area of the city, insisted on these green spaces. But even the most densely populated areas are never far from a park and most streets are tree-lined – as our little estate is. Unlike London, it is relatively quick and easy to get out of the city and be in open countryside. But you don't have to leave the city to be close to green. Even the meanest little flat, whilst it may not have its own garden, will probably look out over a park or a few trees or bushes. And the canal network is a whole world of waterways, much of it flanked by trees, rarely more than a few hundred yards from most of the city roads and streets.[36]

So, right in the heart of the city, the woodland is not far away and it is possible to meander in and out of the woods a dozen times a day, if one is intentional about it. One can walk or cycle in and out of parks and along tree-lined roads. The buses and trains weave their way through trees, the railway often following the canals. Even gazing out of a window into one bush or tree can take one into the heart of the forest, if we are patient enough to let go for a moment or two and enter in. Every single tree is a microcosm of the woods: unique, particular, like a person, yet holding within its branches the promise of the wild, the renewing freedom of the forest, the green wilderness without which we die.

[36] For a delightful and informative account of Birmingham's canal networks, and their wildlife, see Alys Fowler's *Hidden Nature: A Voyage of Discovery* (London: Hodder & Stoughton, 2017).

The traffic between 'woods' and 'fields', the wilds and domesticated spaces

In Berry's poem, the image of the wilds offered happens to be the woods; but of course, woods are not the only native place of withdrawal, renewal, veneration and restoration. As I suggested at the beginning of this chapter, the woods represents the natural wilderness which Berry knows is essential for human sanity and salvation, and can encompass not only trees and forests but also lake, river, beach, mountain, desert. Whether beach, forest, park or desert, the invitation is to the ancient, ancestral, primeval places of fecundity and beauty, the place where the springs of creativity bubble up. This is the place of which the psalmist speaks: 'All my fresh springs are in you' (Psalm 87:7). In truth, a thousand such places exist on the edges of our city streets and suburban gardens, and need not be limited to natural features of the landscape. For many, the art gallery and the concert hall, and perhaps the gym and the swimming pool, will provide places of sanctuary and refreshment, as well as a connection with beauty and an opportunity for physical and spiritual re-creation.

Yet the wilds of the woods still call, beyond the urban spaces where the majority of us now live and call home. Whilst cities expand and the building of roads, railways and airports threatens to engulf more and more of our native wilderness, yet the wild places – so far – endure and remain. Ecological activists, many of them young people, are vocal and resolute in their determination to preserve the wilderness upon which human life depends for its sanity and wisdom, even as we witness the mass extinction of species on a daily basis. To live a responsible, healthy, balanced life, Sabbath teaches us, is to respect and preserve the boundary between the 'fields' and the 'woods', the places of labour and the spaces of our rest, the urban concentration of human industry and commerce and the dense forests, deserts, rivers and oceans which fringe and protect human habitation.

Whether we live in the city or the country, whether we are privileged to tend our own gardens and woods or must seek entry to those tended by others, whether we are old or young, fit and healthy or sick and housebound, we each need to make regular forays into the wild spaces of our world, our imaginations, our dreams, our myths and stories, for our own well-being as well as for the preservation of the beleaguered wilds which are our future and our salvation.

Journal entry

Here I am, having left the six days' world behind, passing through the narrow gate, into the fellowship of leaf and light, of blossom and birdsong. I am back at the monastery, for a long stretch of six days, with my colleagues from Queen's, doing our annual stint of house-sitting for the brothers while they are away on chapter. Even though, in my bag, I have my diary and a long list of all the routine tasks I have to do, I have not looked at them once (nor many of the huge pile of books I have brought with me). Instead, I am re-immersed in my Sabbath book, the severed connection re-established. I glow, my words flow onto the page, out of the silence, out of the body, out of the deep thirst and need to discover and utter my truth.

I need to step apart into the woods, to listen again for the song of my being, the music of my calling. I find it here, in the fields, in the wild green of high summer, in the beauty that is still England, my native land, my deep country roots.

I'm wakened at 4.15 am by the dawn chorus, open the window wide to listen, drift back to sleep with birdsong in my ears, playing through my mind. Earlier, as I came to bed, the sky lit up with lightning, rumbled with thunder, and thick rain pattered down on the dark earth for a long while. I fell asleep to the sweet sound of rain on grateful earth.

Like the earth, I am receiving what is given from above, wide open to the fructifying, generative Spirit. Like the fields, I'm laid bare to the wind rippling and buffeting the grasses, shaking and spreading the pollen. Like the birds,

Sabbath

my soul is awake with the dawn, cooing and chirruping and calling, mad for the bliss of the world's beauty and for being alive in it. Like the sky riven with lightning, rumbling with thunder, I'm crackling and bristling with Pentecostal energy, bursting with new language that is urgent to find its many tongues.

Every year, the seasons become sweeter, more poignant, seem to pass more quickly, yet are rich with memory of all the earlier years of seasons. Now in my sixtieth year, this summer is as sweet as any I can remember, the blossom thicker, the grasses taller, the roses more profligate. After a long, hard winter that lasted well into April, the summer has brought its relief of warmth and growth.

Out of the unmaking, new making. Out of the smouldering ash, new fire. Out of the grief and the dying of love, new love awakening. Out of the forgotten memories, something lost is recovered. Out of what seemed irreparably broken, a new tryst is forged. Out of the body, healing, hopefulness.

I tread the ancient ways to remember where I have come from, who I am, where I am going. I dive into the woods to get lost and to find myself again. I re-enter the Sabbath of the trees.

(1.vi.18)

The apple tree

The apple tree has had a bad press in Christianity,
yet she is the source of all wisdom,
knows how to live into and out of each season.

In spring, she puts out leaves from branches
that are lichened and gnarled. She hides the blackbird's
nest, suckles mistletoe from her chest.

In May, though old and stooped, she puts on bridal froth.
For two short weeks she is more fragrant and lovely
than all the trees in the wood.

In June, lively winds will bring her first fruits down,
hard lozenges scattered on the ground. She knows
she must shed what is good for the gathering of the best.

Sun and wet will ripen her green globes, touch them
    with red.
In late September she'll yield her crop, permit ladders
against her trunk, hands reaching up to bring the fruit
    down.

After six months' work, she'll drop her dusty leaves,
showing her skin, leathered and tough.
She's not afraid to weather the winter. She bides her
    time,

Sabbath

awaits the gardener's pruning hook. After that,
she'll start to put out tiny tentacles,
latching onto air and warmth, smelling the turn.

From her I learn the bearing, the stripping, the rise
and fall, the work of fruiting, the harvest and the letting go.

Questions for reflection and prayer

- *Where, for you, is the woods or the wilds?*
- *Where is the place to which you seek to return for rest, renewal and recreation?*
- *Where is the place where you feel most at home, most truly yourself, the place that tells you who you are in the world?*

It may be a particular landscape, a specific place (a particular church, retreat centre, house, etc.), or it may be something more generic (hills, woods, desert, river, sea). For some, it may be urban rather than rural (city streets, canals, parks, an art gallery, etc.).

In your imagination, go to that place and enter in there. Remember what it feels like to be there – for an hour or so, for a day, for a few days, a week or a season.

- *What does this place remind you of?*
- *What are its gifts to you?*
- *What longings does it rouse in you?*
- *What does it ask of you?*
- *What would it be like to live there always?*

Thinking about the erasure of wilderness in the world invites some broader, political questions:

- *How do you perceive the woods or the wilds to be threatened? What changes have you witnessed in the natural world over your lifetime?*
- *What might the keeping of Sabbath mean in the current context of climate change and impending ecological disaster?*
- *What one thing can you, or a group to which you belong, commit to in order to help protect and preserve some local wilderness space or a particular endangered species?*

Thoughts
and notes

Chapter 3

All my stirring becomes quiet

The invitation to cessation

The Sabbath is not a time to work or fight for the redemption of the world, but a time to anticipate and celebrate its presence already in our midst.

Rosemary Radford Ruether[37]

**I go among trees and sit still.
All my stirring becomes quiet
around me like circles on water.
My tasks lie in their places
where I left them, asleep like cattle.**

[37] *Women-Church: Theology and Practice of Feminist Liturgical Communities* (New York: Harper & Row, 1985):217.

Then what is afraid of me comes
and lives a while in my sight.
What it fears in me leaves me,
and the fear of me leaves it.
It sings, and I hear its song.

Then what I am afraid of comes.
I live for a while in its sight.
What I fear in it leaves it,
and the fear of it leaves me.
It sings, and I hear its song.

After days of labor,
mute in my consternations,
I hear my song at last,
and I sing it. As we sing,
the day turns, the trees move.

Wendell Berry[38]

The undoing and dormancy of Sabbath

In order to enter into the woods, there must be the essential *undoing* of Sabbath: the cessation of our labours and the turning aside into another space, both physical and spiritual – what Jewish tradition names 'the Temple in time'. As Judith Shulevitz puts it, 'The holiness of the Sabbath lies in its being a not-doing in a not-place'. [39] Sabbath is an invitation to pause, to stop doing what we have been doing, however good and meaningful that endeavour, to put our work down for a season, to come to rest and stillness. In one of his early

[38] Sabbaths I, 1979, *This Day:* 7.
[39] Shulevitz, *Sabbath World:* 69.

'Sabbath' poems, Berry describes the leaving of 'labor and load' as he climbs up through the field which his own hard work has 'kept clear'.

> Projects, plans unfulfilled
> Waylay and snatch at me like briars…
>
> I go in pilgrimage
> Across an old fenced boundary
> To wildness without age
> Where, in their long dominion,
> The trees have been left free.

He goes into the woods. As long as he stays in the fields, he knows he will find no rest, for this is the sphere in which 'ceaseless effort seems to be required,/ Yet fails, and spirit tires/ With flesh'[40]. Sabbath requires us to leave the field of our habitual work and enter into the other world of the woods.

In this sense, Sabbath is a boundary we must cross, a liminal space that requires passage. As such, moving in and out of sabbatical space is potentially difficult and requires careful attention, and may even be, for some, a dangerous undertaking. The undoing of Sabbath risks a certain unmaking, and if a person is psychologically fragile this may be a profoundly unsafe place for them to be. From here to there, from the person we think we are to the person we might become; from the person with a name and a job and an identity to one who has nothing to do except walk in the woods, be an idler, a voyager, a discoverer; from clock time to Kairos time; from timetables and lists of things to do to the freefalling hour, the empty page, the undoing and not knowing of Sabbath – this is the passage we are invited to make as we step into sabbatical time and space.

[40] Berry, Sabbaths IV, 1979, *This Day*: 11.

In order to make the passage, it is necessary to stop what we are doing, if only for a momentary pause, and orient towards the new thing, new place, new reality. We must turn our back on one place, one time, one way of doing things, one habitual mode of being who we are, in order to face another. In its own way, this turning (metanoia, conversion) is a miniature death, like the daily death of sleep when we turn from the affairs of consciousness into the non-being of sleep. The forest, we are reminded, is a place of death, even of brutality and violence, and not only of beauty; this is part of its fearsomeness and unknowing. The dark forest is in many ways much closer, more akin, to the anarchic unconscious than it is to the ordered realm of rationality; closer to the mysterious realm of the night than to the broad light of day. The work of the day, the thoughts of the mind, the plans and projects, people and places that occupy our consciousness – these are all well and good in their proper place, but each day we lay them aside, we give our bodies and minds into unconsciousness, that daily practice for death whose spiritual significance was well recognized by our forebears, though largely lost to a contemporary society which sees no value in meditating on our own demise. [41]

The rhythm of the working week is that we rise out of the undoing and remaking of sleep into the tasks of a new day. Not so with Sabbath. On the Sabbath, we awake out of non-doing and unmaking into the wide open space which consists of more of the same. It is not simply that Sabbath is a space for a different *kind* of doing – going to church, say, instead of working in the fields or the laboratory; music-

---

[41] But for an exception, see Janet Morley's wise commentary on mortality in *Our Last Awakening: Poems for living in the face of death* (London: SPCK, 2016). Edward Thomas's poem, 'Lights out', and Morley's commentary on it (pp.74-77) offers a powerful meditation on going into the forest as an assent to death. See also Malcolm Guite, *Love, Remember: 40 poems of loss, lament and hope* (London: Canterbury Press, 2017).

making, painting or needlework instead of cooking or teaching. No, Sabbath is a different kind of space altogether, when we are invited into not-doing, not-knowing, not-intending, not-working, not-pursuing. 'Sabbath honors the necessary wisdom of dormancy', as Wayne Muller puts it. He calls attention to the way in which certain plant species lie dormant during winter in order to bear fruit in the spring. 'A period of rest – in which nutrition and fertility most readily coalesce – is not simply a human psychological convenience; it is a spiritual and biological necessity. A lack of dormancy produces confusion and erosion in the life force.' He continues:

> We, too, must have a period in which we lie fallow, and restore our souls. In Sabbath time we remember to celebrate what is beautiful and sacred; we light candles, sing songs, tell stories, eat, nap, and make love. It is a time to let our work, our lands, our animals lie fallow, to be nourished and refreshed. Within this sanctuary, we become available to the insights and blessings of deep mindfulness that arise only in stillness and time. When we act from a place of deep rest, we are more capable of cultivating what the Buddhists would call right understanding, right action, and right effort. In a complex and unstable world, if we do not rest, if we do not surrender into some kind of Sabbath, how can we find our way, how can we hear the voices that tell us the right thing to do?[42]

The Sabbath pursues us with its own intent – for health, well-being, rest and wholeness – and if we are wise, we succumb to its intentions. As Berry puts it:

[42] Wayne Muller, *Sabbath: Finding Rest, Renewal, and Delight in our Busy Lives* (New York: Bantam, 2000): 7.

The mind that comes to rest is tended
In ways that it cannot intend:
Is borne, preserved, and comprehended
By what it cannot comprehend.

Your Sabbath, Lord, thus keeps us by
Your will, not ours.[43]

Here is how my beloved mentor Maria Harris describes Sabbath in her wise book, *Jubilee Time*:

> Sabbath is … the fundamental pause, stop, and no-saying in Western spirituality. For the ancient Babylonians *sappatu* meant 'the time for quieting the heart' and the Hebrew *shavat* means 'cessation' or 'desistence' from work. Judaism has always made it clear, however, that the cessation and desistance are not pessimistic. Instead, Sabbath's turning away from labor, striving, and anxiety is positive and holy. Out of Sabbath's not-doing, a richer more bountiful kind of doing emerges…
>
> … Sabbath's not-doing means entering a kind of not-knowing or even unknowing, a soul-place where the too-hurried pace of life slows down and another way of walking beckons, one characterized by prayerfulness and awe… not-doing in the way Sabbath suggests is a key that unlocks another world.[44]

God's rest; our hunger for rest

We rest on the Sabbath, opening ourselves up to the possibilities of this other world, because God rests also.

[43] Berry, Sabbaths II, 1979, *This Day*: 9.
[44] Maria Harris, *Jubilee Time: Celebrating Women, Spirit, and the Advent of Age* (Boston: Bantam Books, 1995): 35, 37.

Brueggemann makes much of this notion of God's rest within the creation narrative (Genesis 2:2-3; Exodus 20:11), regarding it as a sign of the character and intention of God for the creation. There is a stark contrast between the order and rhythm of creation, as instituted by the God of Israel, within which rest has a pivotal role, and the competitive, anxious, productivity-driven regime of Pharaoh, which can never let up for a minute.

> God rested. God rested on the seventh day. God did not show up to do more. God absented God's self from the office. God did not come and check on creation in anxiety to be sure it was all working. God has complete confidence in the fruit-bearing, blessing-generating processes of creation that have been instituted. God exhibits no anxiety about the life-giving capacity of creation. God knows the world will hold, the plants will perform, and the birds and the fish and the beasts of the field will prosper. Humankind will govern the earth in a generative way. All will be well, and all manner of thing will be well![45]

What extraordinary trust God displays in God's creation and in humankind – a trust human beings tend not to reciprocate in like manner or degree, not least in our inability to rest. Many of us who call ourselves people of faith seem to be as anxious, compulsively driven and productivity-oriented as Pharaoh, never letting up for a moment in our mindless making of bricks. We seem to fear the giving up of control which Sabbath demands of us, and resist the invitation to cessation as we might resist our own death (we will return to this theme of fear in chapter 5). Yet there is a path 'of leaving the path', as poet David Whyte puts it, which requires such

---

[45] Brueggemann, *Sabbath as Resistance*: 29.

an abdication of control and a 'feral courage' as we face the unknown:

> we hear our own voice
> demanding of ourselves
> a faith in no-path,
> when there is no faith at all.
>
> And moving forward takes feral courage,
> opens the wildest
> most outrageous light of all,
> becomes the hardest path of all.[46]

Yet, whilst we may resist the invitation to cessation, it is not difficult to recognize within ourselves a deep bodily and spiritual hunger for the very rest we refuse. Our bodies and minds manifest in many different forms our deep craving for rest, either in the normal healthy pattern of life well lived or, if we ignore and suppress this deep need, in more and more dysfunctional ways. Either way, the body does not lie, and will become our teacher if we will let it.

Fatigue, illness, boredom, holy idleness

In the normal rhythm of life, we become tired and rest, taking pauses throughout the day to eat and to take exercise or to relax with family and friends. At the end of each day, we take the long sleep without which our bodies and minds cannot replenish. If we ignore this need for rest, we will become more profoundly fatigued, both mentally and physically, we

[46] David Whyte, 'Millennium', *Fire in the Earth* (Morehead, MN: Many Rivers Press, 2002): 6.

will experience an unhealthy level of stress and our bodies are very likely to become ill. Illness is one of the key ways in which our bodies insist on the care and attention they need, especially when we have not been giving them due regard and respect. It is not at all uncommon for busy people to become ill as soon as they relax the normal pressures and stop (maybe one reason why some people don't ever stop). Teachers very often get ill during half-term or school holidays and it is not at all unusual for those who take a longer sabbatical to spend the first part of it – or even most of it – utterly exhausted or ill, as happened to me on my recent sabbatical. Here's a description from my journal of my recent experience of coming away on sabbatical and promptly getting ill:

> I feel I have spent the large part of this time away asleep – emotionally, intellectually and psychically asleep, if not physically asleep (but I've spent hours and hours sleeping, too). My body is greedy for rest, my mind refuses to engage with anything very demanding. I cannot read anything too testing, and I've accomplished nothing on any of the writing projects I am supposed to be working on. I could regard all this as a terrible waste … but there's no point in fighting it. This is how it is. I've needed this time to be ill; to let my body go into torpor, mind switch off, descend into a kind of underground existence where I shuffle about aimlessly – or so it seems – incapable of thinking, creating, taking initiative, seizing the reins… [9.i.15]

Similarly, the mind's need to rest and idle from intense engagement or productivity can manifest in a wide variety of ways: in boredom, ennui, listlessness, forgetfulness, day-dreaming or depression. The early monastic fathers and mothers named this as 'acedia', literally 'not caring', the condition of spiritual dejection, boredom and frustration which, whilst it was generally considered a sin to be resisted, was also recognized as an essential aspect of the solitary life.[47] Adam Phillips, the American psychoanalyst, reflects on the significance of boredom in his essay 'On being bored' in the fabulously titled collection of essays, *On Kissing, Tickling, and Being Bored: Psychoanalytic Essays on the Unexamined Life.* Boredom is a particular feature of childhood, he suggests:

> Every adult remembers, among many other things, the great ennui of childhood, and every child's life is punctuated by spells of boredom: that state of suspended animation in which things are started and nothing begins, the mood of diffuse restlessness which contains that most absurd and paradoxical wish, the wish for a desire …
>
> Boredom is actually a precarious process in which the child is, as it were, both waiting for something and looking for something, in which hope is being secretly negotiated; and in this sense boredom is akin to free-floating attention. In the muffled, sometimes irritable, confusion of boredom the child is reaching to a recurrent sense of emptiness out of which his real desire can crystallize.[48]

Susan Sontag puts it concisely when she suggests that 'boredom is a function of attention',[49] although we may suppose it is its opposite. Adams suggests that boredom, no less than play, is essential to the child's development. Adults

[47] For a recent treatment of acedia, see Kathleen Norris, *Acedia and Me: A Marriage, Monks, and a Writer's Life* (New York: Riverhead Books, 2010).
[48] Adam Phillips, *On Kissing, Tickling, and Being Bored: Psychoanalytic Essays on the Unexamined Life* (Harvard: Harvard University Press, 1993): 68-9.
[49] Susan Sontag, *As Consciousness is Harnessed to Flesh: Journals and Note-books, 1964-1980* (Farrar, Strauss & Giroux, 2012), at https://www.brain-pickings.org/2015/03/16/boredom/ Accessed 3.1.19.

may seek to banish the 'wasted time' of both boredom and play from their highly regulated lives but, if they do, they will likely pay a high price not only in terms of joy and creativity but perhaps at the most basic level of psychological well-being. A life without idling, day-dreaming, staring into space and boredom is a life which does not admit of the possibility of renewal. In one of her most well-known poems, 'The Summer Day', Mary Oliver speaks of being simultaneously 'idle and blessed',[50] a striking phrase which captures something of the quality of Sabbath. I remember sharing this poem with a hard-working Christian woman friend, who was quite shocked at the possibility that idleness could be blessed and that strolling through the fields all day could constitute a form of prayer. For many of us, such blessed idleness has to be cultivated through intentional practice, although there are others who seem to be able to do it quite naturally! The Rule of Life of the Companions of Brother Lawrence contains a commitment to what the Rule calls 'planned neglect', making an intentional choice about 'things we will leave undone or postpone, so that instead of being oppressed by a clutter of unfinished jobs, we think out our priorities under God, and then accept, without guilt or resentment, the fact that much we had thought we ought to do, we must leave'. [51]

There is the Sabbath of planned neglect and deliberate, holy idleness, for sure – but Sabbath is not so much part of our orderly, planned routines as it is God's interruption of them, a gift from beyond – not always welcome, though always benign – which relativizes and scrutinizes all our projects and plans. There is a prayer by the Australian cartoonist Leunig, which begins: 'God give us rain when

[50] Mary Oliver, 'The Summer Day', *New and Selected Poems* (Boston: Beacon Press, 1992): 94.
[51] In Christina Rees, *Feast & Fast: Food for Lent and Easter* (London: Darton, Longman & Todd, 2010): 28.

we expect sun. Give us music when we expect trouble. Give us tears when we expect breakfast,[52] and this may bring us closer to the spirit of Sabbath. For Sabbath is a feature of God's Kairos time rather than Chronos time, and therefore always has an element of the unexpected, the gratuitous about it. However much it is part and parcel of the expected order of the week, Sabbath ushers in a space of grace in which we cannot predict what will happen. Precisely because the Sabbath requires us to let go our habitual control and give over to the non-being of God's Kairos moment, it opens us up to encounter with the depths which is both awesome and fearful. It is the opportunity for creation to enter into God's rest for a season, rather than for God to partake of our little vacations from industry and endeavour. The scale and scope of the Sabbath are divine rather than human, and this is part of what makes it fearful as well as profoundly rejuvenating.

Whether planned, spontaneous or serendipitous, welcome or resisted, there is no human life that will not have its measure of idleness, boredom, fatigue or listlessness, when the ship is in the doldrums, at sea with no breath of wind available to fill the sails and drive it forward. Life can become devoid of passion, jouissance, the erotic dimension – for long stretches of time, even for years. All one's desires dry up. Food tastes the same, there's no desire for sex or for anything in particular. Most, if not all of us, will fall ill, become depressed, waste opportunities, get stuck in dead-end jobs or have to work through difficult or failed relationships. Our early dreams and aspirations may be unmade or never fulfilled; our achievements and successes may subsequently unravel. All of us, as we move closer to death, will have to relinquish much that we have prized and that has given our lives meaning. Whether we see such challenges as marks of failure or hidden opportunities for

[52] Leunig, *A Common Prayer: A cartoonist talks to God* (Oxford: Lion, 1997), no page numbers.

soul-making may, in large part, depend on the everyday practices that hold our lives in place and shape our values as well as our hours. The practice of Sabbath as an intentional embrace of 'uselessness' may teach us to how to approach all that seems difficult and without meaning in our lives in a spirit of hopeful trust. Listen to Cheryl Strayed:

> The useless days will add up to something. The shitty waitressing jobs. The hours writing in your journal. The long meandering walks. The hours reading poetry and story collections and novels and dead people's diaries and wondering about sex and God and whether you should shave under your arms or not. These things are your becoming. [53]

The gift of Sabbath

The great gift of Sabbath is to teach us that cessation, not-doing, silence and the pause are at the heart of the rhythm of work and life. There is an essential pause at the heart of all creative work and endeavour: the silence which is integral to music, to poetry and liturgy; the wide margins around the page when we are reading or writing; all that is excised from the poem or the painting, what is left out in order for what is there to breathe. I used to think the gaps in between work were empty space, wasted time or at most, concessions to the weakness of mind and body: all that counted for work was the conscious, explicit attention to the task – and I'd feel guilty or secretly triumphant that I'd managed to escape the burden of work when I was away from my desk. Now I've come to see that the rests and pauses, the moments

[53] Cheryl Strayed, *Tiny Beautiful Things: Advice on Love and Life from Dear Sugar* (Vintage, 2012): x.

or hours when the mind is idling, the day-dreaming, the walk along the beach and the long hours of sleep are, in fact, an essential part of the work. We are not machines which can go on mindlessly, hour after hour, day after day, but human beings with our mysterious rhythms of ebb and flow, receiving and giving, ingesting and out-pouring. 'It is in vain', the psalmist says, 'that you rise up early and go late to rest, eating the bread of anxious toil, for God gives sleep to his beloved' (Psalm 127:2).

Just as the seed must sink down into the dark of the soil and rest undisturbed before it will germinate; just as the kneaded dough must be left, covered, in a warm place to rise; just as mammals hibernate during the cold months of winter, storing up energy for the approaching season; just as fields must be left fallow for a year in order to replenish their nutrients; just as the writer or painter or musician must leave their work for many days or weeks in order for the evolution of the new creation to emerge – so all life partakes of the rhythm of dormancy and rest.

Sabbath is the breathing space in our labours, the pause in and before and after the music, the clearing in the woods through which the light comes, the empty dark hours of night in which our minds and bodies regenerate themselves and God gives gifts, treasures of darkness, to God's beloved. Sabbath is, indeed, the hidden heartbeat of our lives.

Living the hours

David Whyte speaks of the importance of 'living the hours [of work] spaciously, where we actually have a relationship with silence and timelessness', in contrast to 'working only to do':

Without the timelessness of the hours, celebration, rhythm and anticipation disappear from our work life; we lose the sense of music in our lives. As if a symphony, with all its rest, attenuated beats, and rhythms, suddenly had all silence between the notes removed, leaving the notes undifferentiated, crushed and bruised, each sound pressed into the next. Without silence work is not music, but a mechanical hum, like an old refrigerator, the white background noise corroding our attempts at a real conversation and only noticed in the reverberating kitchen, when it finally brings itself to a stop.[54]

Whyte's concept of 'living the hours' brings to mind the Church's liturgy of the hours, enshrined in particular by monastic communities which live out the ancient sevenfold offices (Matins, Lauds, Prime, Terce, Sext, None, Vespers and Compline) or some shorter variant of it. The hours of prayer (some of them very short, the so-called 'little offices' or 'minor hours' of Terce, Sext and None consisting of a few brief psalms, a hymn, the kyrie and the Lord's Prayer and generally lasting only about ten minutes) punctuate each day and night with an unceasing, dependable regularity around which the whole day and night are organized. They function as repeated Sabbath pauses within each day, interrupting the routine tasks of the day or more important, even critical matters, relativizing all human activity in the light of the primary calling of the monastic to prayer. This traditional sevenfold office has been adapted and shortened for use by more active religious communities and by third order oblates living the rule of the community in the world. Anglican liturgy, with its daily celebration of morning and evening prayer, is a pared down version of the monastic offices and many modern Christian communities have

[54] David Whyte, *Crossing the Unknown Sea: Work and the Shaping of Identity* (London: Penguin, 2002):174

developed their own versions of this, from Taizé to Iona, the Northumberland Community and new monastic communities. Many Christians find a commitment to some kind of daily rhythm of short times of prayer, in solidarity with other members of a wider community doing the same thing, to be a helpful way of practising regular pauses within the day, even if they are very short and need to be taken whilst travelling to work on the train, or in a lunch or coffee break. Doing this in communion with others, including monks and nuns in monasteries, also reminds us that prayer, like Sabbath, is never a private affair but takes place within the wider Christian community. Our own practice, however faltering and irregular, is upheld by the faithful prayers and Sabbath-keeping of others.

Meals themselves, of course, may function as another form of regular pause within the day, and whilst regular, shared mealtimes seem to be victim of an increasingly hectic pace of life, with many adults and children eating on the move, or in front of the TV or computer screen, there is an increasing move to recover 'slow food', alongside many other forms of 'slow' practice.[55] The preparation, as well as the eating of food, can become a slow, deliberate, contemplative practice, where the aim is to relish the physical, sensual engagement with raw food stuffs as they are prepared, both honouring and enjoying the colour, texture, smell and beauty of grains, pulses, vegetables, fruit, fish and flesh. The practice of cooking and eating as a deliberate, prayerful activity includes the ethical commitment to choose organic, wholefood and fairly traded produce, where possible, and/

[55] For more on the slow food movement, see https://www.slowfood.com/ and https://www.slowfood.org.uk/ and many other local websites. See also John Lane, *Timeless Simplicity: Creative living in a consumer society* (Dartington: Green Books, 2001) and Carl Honoré, *In Praise of Slowness: Challenging the Cult of Speed* (New York: HarperCollins, 2004) (chapter 4 is on slow food).

or to grow one's own food to the extent that this is possible (and much is possible even in the smallest of gardens or in window boxes and planters).

However we do it, there are multiple ways of 'living the hours' mindfully, gratefully and consciously, rather than speeding through the day on automatic pilot in a rush against the clock. The invitation to pause at numerous points in the day is part of God's invitation to Sabbath, whether it is to rest, to eat, to gather with colleagues at work, to pray, to walk or take other forms of exercise, to weed or plant or prune in the garden, to do other kinds of physical work (housecleaning, cooking, ironing can all be forms of contemplative practice if we regard them as such), or to play with our children or pets. I live with two cats, as well as a human partner, and one of the things we say about the cats is that they make us laugh every single day of our lives, even the most terrible days of death and tragedy. They live by their own rhythms, apparently feeling no need to work for a livelihood (they don't even have to hunt for food, since we provide it for them), permitting themselves long stretches of sleep, and demanding human attention and worship at regular intervals through the day as their natural birthright. We gladly give it to them, and return to our own tasks with a smile on our faces and a lighter step. However we find and make them, such pauses in the day will sustain and support our work, and remind us that we are more than the sum of our labours, and that we are made for rest and play, for prayer and contemplation, as well as for work.

Journal entry

I've always been plagued by long periods of illness or of exhaustion, throughout my life, from childhood onwards, and in adulthood often by a mixture of the two, chronic fatigue syndrome representing the epitome of the condition. I've come to accept that I'm likely always to live in the tension between intense engagement, feeling and creativity, on the one hand, and periods of emptiness, ennui and fatigue on the other. I'm like my mother, a passionate Celt who feels things too intensely and wants too much out of life. I'll never disabuse myself entirely of this passionate nature, nor would I want to, since it is the source of my energy, creativity, love of life and desire to connect. But it can cost me – and doubtless others who have to live or work with me closely – dear.

I've known others – mainly men, it has to be said – who seem able to write and produce consistently, working at a steady pace, day in, day out, week in, week out, even year in, year out, without the need for disengagement or holiday. I think of L. who would go on 'holiday' largely to write his next book, rather than to enjoy living for a week or two free from the demands of work. I might envy such people, but I can't ape them. I'm not like that and, however much I try to temper the more excessive extremes of my temperament so that I don't lurch from height to depth as I might once have done, I need to allow for these periods, which may be prolonged, when I'm not able to engage creatively, when I have to lie low, let the ship rest at anchor, allow the land to be untilled, go to seed.

Sabbath

This theme – of learning to live with a deep need for rest, withdrawal and retreat – is one that recurs continually in my journals over the years. Here is a typical entry:

I'm at Glasshampton monastery for 24 hours, driving out yesterday after a session with my spiritual director, staying up in the light-filled room above the chapel, looking out over harvested fields. In all the years I've been coming here, I don't think I've ever been here in this season of late summer. The hollyhocks are high in the front border; a blaze of sweet-smelling lilies greets one at the door. In the back garden, the herbaceous border is splendid and lacy pink hydrangea give a splash of colour. The big Bramley apple tree is heavy with huge fruit.

This is a place I come to for wisdom amidst the welter of words and tasks before me; for water in a time of thirst; stillness where my anxious heart is restive; orientation when I have momentarily lost my bearings.

How can I be so tired and empty-headed, so physically fragile, when I have just had two weeks' holiday? Perhaps precisely because I've just had two weeks' holiday! My body and mind have let go utterly, I've come to a place of cessation and rest. And now I'm craving more, more, want to let go deeper into the abyss of thoughtlessness, mindlessness, the dreaming state of long summer nights that births images, poems, the creative impulse – though in its own time, only in its own time. My body craves sleep and sleep and sleep. My mind simply wants to be empty.

I'm laying aside my own claim on the day. If I do nothing more than pray this day and nap all the hours between, it will have been a day well spent.

Annie Dillard, in Pilgrim at Tinker Creek, asserts (as only she can): 'Experiencing the present purely is being emptied and hollow; you catch grace as a man fills his cup under a waterfall.'[56] So, here I am, emptied and hollow, not through my own choice or design, but simply how my body finds me – ripe for grace, hanging about under that waterfall that is Spirit with my little cup, looking to be filled/drenched.

(28.viii.15)

---

[56] Anne Dillard, *Pilgrim at Tinker Creek* (London: Picador, 1976): 80.

Aldeburgh

There is no need
            to write a poem
                        read a book
    though this is what I came for.

Sufficient to walk
            every morning
                        every evening
    the flat pebbled shore

notice colours
            the dun, the dappled, the dazzling

taste spray on my lips
            let the body
                        fill up with tiredness.

It is enough
            to sleep

                        the long dreamless sleep

no poems
            disturbing the ear.
                        Then wake
    to wander again
            on the shore
                        see what patent

All my stirring becomes quiet

God has mixed from his palette

                               freshly squeezed

sky washed clean by darkness

                               worked again into

poetry my eyes

                    have never beheld

                                  until now.

An ordinary life

I want to wash dishes for a year,
peel potatoes, make pies and cakes,
kneel in the earth and pull weeds.
Take time to pray, read, give myself
to poems.

Who made this crazy life,
anyway, of scrabbling and pushing
and sweating as you tread a highwire
pitched between mountains, not knowing
when you'll fall, legs freewheeling in mid air?

You did. Nobody but you.
And nobody else can unmake it.

Questions for reflection and prayer

- *Where or what, for you, is Sabbath rest, pause, cessation?*
- *When and how do you stop in order to practise the 'not-doing' of Sabbath?*
- *Do you find this easy or difficult and, if difficult, do you know why?*
- *What role does silence play in your life and in your prayer? Is it something you crave and welcome or something you find difficult and try to avoid?*
- *How do you respond to the notions of 'blessed idleness' (Mary Oliver) and 'planned neglect' (Companions of Brother Lawrence)? How might you practise these within your own rule of life?*
- *Do you ever 'fast' from your computer, mobile phone, emails and so on? If so, how do you experience this? What are its benefits and drawbacks? If not, is this something you could try?*
- *How might the invitation to Sabbath rest manifest in your life in hidden ways – for example, through illness, exhaustion, boredom, dreams or longing?*

Thoughts and notes

Chapter 4

It sings and I hear its song

The invitation to encounter

The Sabbath (of the cosmos and God) as receptivity is found in the shared nature of love, the medium of mutual penetration of selves that becomes the true source and end of enjoyment.

Elaine Padilla[57]

> I go among trees and sit still.
> All my stirring becomes quiet
> around me like circles on water.
> My tasks lie in their places
> where I left them, asleep like cattle.

[57] *Divine Enjoyment: A Theology of Passion and Exuberance* (Fordham University Press, 2014): 73.

Then what is afraid of me comes
and lives a while in my sight.
What it fears in me leaves me,
and the fear of me leaves it.
It sings, and I hear its song.

Then what I am afraid of comes.
I live for a while in its sight.
What I fear in it leaves it,
and the fear of it leaves me.
It sings, and I hear its song.

After days of labor,
mute in my consternations,
I hear my song at last,
and I sing it. As we sing,
the day turns, the trees move.

Wendell Berry[58]

Sabbath as relational and conversational space

As we take the risk of crossing the border into the sabbatical space and allow our minds and bodies to become still, to cease their endless round of doing, we may hear the invitation to encounter: to engage with the other, whether that other be another place, another person, another book or idea, another reality, another time. Perhaps we are afraid of the emptiness, the loneliness of cessation; we fear it will be an arid space, there will be nothing or no one there in the solitude of our not-doing except our lonely selves, whom we avoid at all costs. Yet, can we but trust it, the Sabbath space

[58] Sabbaths I, 1979, *This Day*: 7.

is, in fact, a profoundly relational and conversational space, a space in which we are invited to encounter the other, as well as aspects of ourselves which we frequently ignore or neglect – both of whom come with gifts, though they may be unexpected and unfamiliar ones.

The 'no-saying' of Sabbath is not essentially negative, though we may sometimes experience it as such. Rather, it is in order that a larger and more hospitable 'yes' can be uttered to the other. As Wayne Muller puts it,

> by saying no to making some things happen, deep permission arises for other things to happen. When we cease our daily labor, other things – love, friendship, prayer, touch, singing, rest – can be born in the space created by our rest. Walking with a friend, reciting a prayer, caring for children, sharing bread and wine with family and neighbors – those are intimate graces that need precious time and attention.[59]

At the heart of Berry's 1979 Sabbath poem, in the mysterious second and third stanzas, we find evoked an encounter with the other. The poem describes the drawing near of something or someone of whom one is afraid or who is afraid of the walker in the woods (I will return to the theme of fear in the next chapter); the identity of the creature remains mysterious. The imagery here is not so mysterious, I came to realize some years into knowing this poem well, though the poem seems to make it so. Berry has in mind, I think, the hidden presence of animals and birds in a wood that only permit themselves to be seen by the human intruder when that human being learns to become very still and quiet, to merge with the woods and become part of the environment rather than a loud, disruptive threat to other species. The

[59] Muller, *Sabbath*: 29-30.

poet here is a bird watcher, removing himself from sight and sound in the hide, remaining still and alert, all his energies focused on the horizon of the woods and the hidden life that may reveal itself. In time, the watcher is rewarded, the birds appear and sing their song. The poet listens, receives the gift of the birdsong, and perhaps, too, the gift of other creatures emerging from the undergrowth: deer, rabbit, fox, squirrel or mouse.

Writing about discipleship, Rowan Williams speaks about it as 'a state of awareness' characterized by waiting and expectancy, an endeavour to be in the place where the Master lives in order that the disciple may be changed in the Master's presence. Williams likens the cultivation or practice of such awareness – another way of speaking of prayer – to the activity of a bird watcher.[60] 'The experienced birdwatcher, sitting still, poised, alert, not tense or fussy, knows that this is the kind of place where something extraordinary suddenly bursts into view. I've always loved that image of prayer as birdwatching. You sit very still because something is liable to burst into view, and sometimes, of course it means a long day of sitting in the rain with nothing very much happening.'[61] This process of 'living in this sort of expectancy,'[62] as Williams describes it, seems to me close to the kind of openness to encounter which I am describing as at the heart of Sabbath.

In Berry's poem, there is no encounter with the human other; at least no human other is overtly present in the poem. Berry leaves the world of human relationships and work behind in order to enter the woods as a solitary man, to enter into renewed relationship with the natural

[60] Rowan Williams, *Being Disciples: Essentials of the Christian Life* (London: SPCK, 2016): 3-4.

[61] Williams, *Being Disciples*: 4.

[62] Williams, *Being Disciples*: 5.

realm – the woods, the water, the creatures living within the woods. Yet in many other poems, Berry explores his profound commitment to, and contract with, the human landscape which remains eclipsed in this, and indeed, in most of his Sabbath poems. When one reads the Sabbath poems alongside his other poems and essays, it becomes abundantly clear that his life commitment as both farmer and writer is rooted in a covenant with a particular tract of land, handed on to him in trust by earlier generations, and with a particular community of people – neighbours, immediate family, local villagers and townsfolk. Above all, Berry's life as writer, poet, critic and activist is rooted in his covenant relationship with his wife, his life partner. 'The country of marriage', as one of his collections of poems is named, is where he lives. [63]

When he enters the woods as a solitary, Berry does not leave behind the tight mesh of relationships and covenant commitments that sustain his writing and his work – and nor do we. If anything, these relationships become clearer and surer in the temporary withdrawal from them, their contours and texture revealed in sharper, simpler outline. The creatures of the woods which draw near in the poem can stand for other relationships and persons who, in like manner, draw near to the solitary watcher, even in their absence. This is quite common an experience amongst those who go on retreat or travel away from their familiar surroundings and relationships; the absence allows one to recognize more clearly than in normal life how dependent one is on those few others who make up the close inner circle of intimates with whom one shares oneself most deeply. In the silence and solitariness of retreat, we have more time than usual to become aware of the many others with whom

---

[63] Wendell Berry, *The Country of Marriage* (Berkeley, CA: Counterpoint, 2013, 4th edition).

we are connected, to think about them and pray for them. They are not absent, but present in what may feel like a *more* rather than less real presence.

Sabbath as social and intimate space

In Jewish tradition and practice, Sabbath is an essentially social rather than solitary space. It is a time for gathering in family and friendship groups, for eating and talking. It celebrates the coming together of one's closest kith and kin, and if it is a resting, it is a resting in community. The Sabbath begins at sundown with the Sabbath meal, when the woman of the household lights the Sabbath candles and recites the Sabbath blessing over the meal. It is a time for recognizing the sacredness of what we often take for granted: the security of home, the comfort of ordinary things (furniture, furnishings, crockery, cutlery we have chosen or been given, all of which have their own particular associations and memories), the givenness of our most intimate relationships, the nourishment of food and the gladness of wine, the beauty of candlelight and flowers on the table, the cherishing of loved ones and the pleasure of conversation. All of these are integral to Sabbath, and they are received as blessings of God and signs of God's covenant faithfulness. There is no division between spiritual and sensual, ordinary and sacred. All is sacred, all is blessed.

Sabbath is a time for *relishing*: a word that can apply equally to food, sex and time itself. Settle back, Sabbath says, breathe deeply, ease into your chair, look into the faces of those who sit with you – your child, your lover, your mother or father, your dear friend – and realize how much you love them and depend upon them. Take time to relish them, as you relish the good food and wine, the candlelight, the flowers, the cats curled up in the corner, the drawing in of the light. Don't rush or bolt your food, give it the respect and time it deserves. Eat slowly. Chew. Masticate. Savour the textures, aromas and flavours. And relish human conversation. Tell the story of your day, your week, your consolations and desolations. And listen to the stories of others. Expect to be surprised, entertained, enlivened. Find good things to talk about. Don't criticize or complain. Go out of your way to praise and celebrate – including what is imperfect, incomplete and most wounded. 'Try to praise the mutilated world.'[64]

Sabbath invites us to rest in one another. Rest in the light of your lover's eyes or your child's smile. Watch and enjoy the way bodies unwind and visibly relax over food and wine and talk. Get lost in the meandering paths of tall stories, ridiculous jokes, long-repeated memories or holiday reminiscences. Maybe there will be sadness to be acknowledged too, but bundle the hurts and tragedies into the Sabbath blanket of blessing. After the long, slow, leisurely meal, lie back on the couch in each other's arms, making a lap for the cats. Luxuriate in week's end. Later, go to bed and rest again in each other's bodies. Make love, whether you have sex or not. Make an ending to the day that is loving and kind. Come home to yourself and to each other in the blessed rest of this Sabbath. How would it be if every week ended and began like this? Why should it not?

Making love is one of the sacred duties of Sabbath, according to the Talmud and the rabbis. In some sects, it is traditional to make love four times during Sabbath.[65] This pleasure in physical intimacy is also expressed in the traditional blessing that parents give their children at the Sabbath meal, placing a hand on the head of each child

---

[64] The title of Adam Jagajewski's poem. At https://www.poetryfoundation. org/poems/57095/try-to-praise-the-mutilated-world-56d23a3f28187 Accessed 4.1.19.
[65] Muller, *Sabbath*: 31.

and reciting a blessing. The joy of Sabbath rest is not an ascetic withdrawal from human community, intimacy and love, but a cherishing and renewal of that love, expressed in touch. Strict Sabbatarian legalism, within both Judaism and Christianity, lost sight of this celebration of the sensual and the physical so that the Sabbath become an endurance test of boredom and discomfort, in which anything pleasurable – the playing of games, dancing, music, theatre or cinema – was outlawed, replaced by a very limited repertoire of permitted activities. Reading (so long as it was reading of the 'right' kind of book – nothing racy, sexy or secular), sewing, knitting and 'sacred conversation' were allowed. This is a travesty of Sabbath and a denial of the pleasure at its heart.

The metaphor of conversation

Conversation is a core expression of Sabbath in any Jewish household, particularly around the Sabbath meal, and I want to suggest that 'conversation' is a helpful metaphor for a grasping of the relational creativity of Sabbath. Of course, conversation may happen at any mealtime but the pressures of the working week often dictate that meals are perfunctory and, in many households, family members are not able to gather on a daily basis, differing work schedules necessitating different eating patterns. Or when families do eat together, it may be in front of the TV when the primary focus of attention is on the screen, rather than on each other. Sabbath invites participation in the family meal in an altogether different kind of way. The tasks of the week are set aside, the welcoming spaciousness of Sabbath creates a space for leisurely eating and conversation. The conversation is not functional but for pleasure and recreation, with time for long drawn-out stories, reminiscences, jokes and banter. It may break into song, and laughter usually punctuates the flow. So may tears.

Sabbath is a conversational space, which includes conversation with our selves, a listening to the self and its longings which we may not have time or space for in ordinary life; but also conversation with the other. Sabbath offers us the space for the extended conversation, the unexpected conversation, the serendipitous conversation, the surprising conversation: the conversation for its own sake that is not seeking to persuade anyone, produce anything or pre-empt anything. Those of us who have been fortunate to enjoy sabbaticals may have had the experience of many such conversations over the lunch or dinner table, with friends, strangers, visitors both far and near, at home or in far flung spaces. This was certainly part of the deep giftedness of my time at Vaughan Park.

Sabbatical space gives us the opportunity to range both widely and deeply in our reading, thinking and conversation. The constraints of having to read or think for a particular task are removed (even if we *are* engaged in a particular project, those constraints are lessened or lifted for a while), and this allows a different kind of engagement. I find reading on sabbatical quite different from reading in my normal routine of work where I am generally reading *for* a particular, often quite imminent, purpose: to prepare a lecture, to offer feedback to a student, to write a sermon or to engage in the work of some committee. Any other reading – for pleasure or for nourishment – has to be fitted around this primary reading, and often gets squeezed out in consequence. On sabbatical, by contrast, I can read both deeply and widely. I can give whole days to reading, stopping only for food or prayer or sleep, or to walk the beach – letting the words and images drift, mingle, settle more deeply. I am given permission to choose apartness, withdrawal: to go into the inner chamber, shut the door and settle down with my book and notebook. Not to evade the conversation with the other, but precisely in order that I may enter into it more deeply, more fully, more wholeheartedly. I can follow up the footnotes, rather than just keeping to the main path of the book or article I'm reading.

I love the opportunity to read widely and eclectically, to engage with ideas and books and people I wouldn't previously have considered. At one time, I would have thought I could only justify my academic existence by concentrating on 'serious' scholarly texts, and would have felt guilty for indulging in 'frivolous' reading or anything 'off-piste'. Now, I positively relish the creative interplay of seemingly unrelated books, ideas, fields of study and disciplines meeting, mingling and interacting. Isn't this what we mean by inter-disciplinarity? This was part of the genius of the Vaughan Park scholars' gathering, which brought together scholars from different continents, disciplines, cultural and social backgrounds, inviting and allowing our many diverse interests, topics and fields to meet and mingle in conversation. The surprising, unexpected conversation is often the source of insight and fresh perspective that would never have been given if we had stuck with one topic or perspective or field of enquiry. It is precisely the meeting and intermingling of apparently unrelated fields or questions that can lead to the creative frisson of new thought.

'Conversation' is a more helpful model of the kind of community envisaged by Sabbath, I want to suggest, than 'dialogue', a notion which has been powerful in theologies of inter-religious encounter. 'Conversation' is wider and more inclusive than dialogue, which suggests encounter between two. There is no limit to the number of people who can be engaged in conversation, nor does 'conversation' presuppose equality of power amongst those who talk. 'Dialogue' can have a rather limited, cerebral connotation; it may suggest learned discourse between experts who are equally knowledgeable, whereas conversation can be about anything and everything and can be conducted by friends and children as well as adults. No-one is precluded.[66]

The radical inclusivity of Sabbath

We are reminded here of how, in Scripture, the Sabbath is intended for every member of the community – the slave as well as the head of the household, the children as well as the adults – and for animals and land as well, who are also somehow to be brought into the conversation. Nor is there any kind of boundary around the subject of conversation. Conversation between friends, colleagues, children or those who have never met before but find themselves thrown together by circumstance, can – and usually does – range freely and widely around an extraordinary array of topics, many of which may not appear to have much, if any, logical connection. This is part of the beauty, as well as the risk, of conversation: we never know where it is going to go next or what it will turn up. Good conversation, like good wine or a good book, is complex and many-textured. Every conversation is unique and unrepeatable and, of course, much that happens in a conversation is not at the level of words or the verbal. Similarly, the experience of Sabbath is many-levelled and richly textured. Sabbath is not a utilitarian concept, even if we can point to obvious and good outcomes of a regular rest from labour. Like

[66] I am, of course, simplifying a complex debate about the conditions for interreligious dialogue here and refer readers to recent publications for a more extensive and nuanced discussion. See, for example, Catherine Cornille, *The Im-Possibility of Interreligious Dialogue* (Independent Publishers Group, 2008), Alan Race & Paul M. Hedges (eds.), *Christian Approaches to Other Faiths* (London: SCM, 2013) and Ray Gaston, *Faith, Hope and Love: Interfaith Engagement as Practical Theology* (London: SCM, 2017).

conversation, it is entered into for its own sake, not for any particular outcome. Like conversation, it is a wide open space which can lead into the unexpected, the serendipitous and the unforeseen.

Wendell Berry has a wonderful poem entitled 'To the unseeable animal',[67] presumably sparked off by his daughter's comment (which appears as the epigraph to the poem): 'I hope there's an animal somewhere that nobody has ever seen. And I hope nobody ever sees it'. The poem is a kind of prayer addressed to the 'Being, whose flesh dissolves/ at our glance', the one who is

> ... always here,
> dwelling in the oldest sycamores,
> visiting the faithful springs
> when they are dark and the foxes
> have crept to their edges.

The poet imagines coming upon pools in the forest or waking deep in the woods and knowing that the unseeable animal has been there, resting, 'watching the little fish', gazing upon the poet as he slept – seeing yet never seen.

The unseeable animal is, for me, an image of the inexhaustible conversation that Sabbath both permits and invites. There is no limit to the creatures that may come close in the Sabbath clearing in the woods and reveal themselves, watching us, resting with us, singing to us. We will never exhaust the possible visitations of these creatures: the creatures of our dreams, the creatures of our imagination, as well as the real creatures and persons (cats, dogs, birds, horses, family members, friends) with whom we live and move and have to do, who we never fully know and always have more to reveal of themselves, and who may remain, in

---

[67] 'To the unseeable animal', *New Collected Poems*: 161.

some significant respects, 'unseeable'. Having lived now, for many years, with cats, I recognize what others who live with cats say (I don't call them 'cat owners', since no human being owns a cat!), that they deign to dwell with us and share their life with us, yet remind us in countless subtle (and not-so-subtle) ways that they possess an unalienable right to their own inner, as well as outer, lives, which we may presume to see but actually remain largely hidden from human eyes. At the end of all our conversations, they seem to say, there will always be the unseeable animal, the creature beyond our glimpse or comprehension, very present in its unassailable otherness, just out of our field of vision, beckoning us into its darkness.

Sabbath conversation is the antithesis of the kind of tired, bored, deeply defensive talking (I won't call it 'conversation' because it is not any form of genuine converse) we can sometimes get into with those we know well and live with. It is easy to lose genuine interest in each other, to come to think we know exactly what the other person is going to say and to lapse into certain cycles of repetition where we go round and round in circles, there is nothing new, and the grooves get deeper and more entrenched.

By contrast, Sabbath conversation takes place on the first day of the week, on the cusp of the new world order created by God, in which everything is miraculously original and fresh from the Word, including language itself. Sabbath invites us to re-enter Eden where we see everything with entirely new eyes. We may be sitting down at the same table with the same old partner, mother, brother, uncle, niece or neighbour whom we have supped with hundreds of times before. We may be eating roast chicken and apple pie for the thousandth time. We may think we know exactly what Aunt Edna or cousin Joe is going to say, we've heard these stories countless times before, we know the punch line that's coming. We've prayed these Sabbath prayers so often, repeated the well-worn lines week in, week out, they're imprinted on our minds and bodies.

But look! This is the first day of the week, the first day of creation on which the world is reborn, washed clean. Look at the people around you at this table as if you've never seen them before – as indeed you never *have* seen them before as they are here, now, today. Regard them with as much awe and wonder as you would the unseeable creature whose face you'll never look upon in the forest clearing. Sabbath is the invitation to origination, to newness, to hope, not in some far-off, never-never land of the future, but right here in the place of the all-too-familiar, the repeated actions and cycles amongst the ones we think we know so well – as well as the back of our hand or the face of our child – and yet who we never really know at all, who can always surprise us with their ineluctable mystery.

The uncanny thing about ritual is that it's as old as the hills, as familiar as a family meal, but it's never exactly the same twice over. It's 'new every morning' and evening, with the endless capacity to re-create us. That's why we keep on doing it.

Journal entries

'Blessed are those... who have set their
hearts on pilgrimage'
(Psalm 84:6, New Zealand Prayerbook)

My heart is on pilgrimage, seeking the paths to God in new places, seeking the way, the homeward road.

Although I am so far from home, and everything here is new, it does not feel strange to me. The landscape and seascape, in particular, feel very much kin – resonant of the Celtic landscape that is deeply in my blood and bones. I tramp the shore here – one day in glorious sun, the next in rain – and it could be the beach on Barra, or Northern Burrows or the cliffs at Kettleness.

3.15 pm. I'm sitting on the shore at Granny's Bay, just half a mile further on from Long Bay, in a thin summer shirt and three-quarter length trousers. Bare arms, bare legs. It is like a balmy summer's day. The light is completely stunning, utterly dazzling, and the views all around the coast in either direction and across Hauraki Gulf are fantastic. I'm almost ringed around by coastline, in a great sweeping arc, like a horseshoe, and where the land ends on either side, in the middle, in the gap, rears a large, mountainous island, so there is a sense of being completely ringed around.

I came this same path yesterday, in persistent rain, the paths and vegetation dripping – me too! – and it was still beautiful. Yesterday, I met no one on the path.

Sabbath

Today, from first light (around 6.45 am), people have been arriving, and the beach, park and path are busy with couples, families, groups, individuals, walking their dogs, sun-bathing, swimming, boating, barbequing and picnicking...

The chapel at Vaughan Park is an extraordinary architectural space, like an upturned boat balancing on the cliff edge, and already I'm loving praying in it; loving the New Zealand Prayerbook, which is so much more inclusive, creative and free-spirited than anything the Church of England has produced or one could imagine our Liturgical Commission producing (sadly). It makes a deliberate policy of using inclusive language, not only for humanity, but also for God; no 'he's anywhere in sight, though masculine metaphors such as Lord, King, Father, etc., remain. But alongside them, the deliberate inclusion of maternal/feminine metaphors and gender non-specific terms such as Creator, Redeemer, Sustainer. And of course, it's bi-lingual, English and Maori, with Maori prayers and chants alongside material from, for instance, Jim Cotter, and many lovely prayers, poems and resources that enrich the rather simple, unstuffy liturgy.

(3.v.09)

As if yesterday afternoon weren't perfect enough, on my way back up the beach today, a woman stopped me and pointed out to the sea – a school of dolphins, I don't know how many of them – five, six, seven, eight – was leaping and cavorting in the water, their black fins glistening where they cut the water, every so often diving into the air. I grabbed my binoculars and gazed and gazed for a good five minutes or so, in a kind of dazed ecstasy: not only that such beautiful creatures should have appeared at that moment and danced, so it seemed, for me, but also that that woman had thought to stop me, because if she hadn't, I wouldn't have seen them, wouldn't have known they were there.

(4.v.09)

For the first time since I've been here, the sea is roaring! The rain is lashing down – nothing new there – but there's also a wind up, and the sea is grey with white caps on all the waves. I've just been out to walk along the shore after Morning Prayer and got absolutely soaked – but it's wonderful, hugely exhilarating.

Yesterday I walked a fair mile or so in the city; after the eucharist here, and coffee and muffins, I took the bus in and walked across town to the Domain, Auckland's largest park, at the top of which is the huge and imposing Museum. There are three floors of artefacts, and in almost three hours I only managed the first of them: a fascinating and powerful display of Polynesian and Maori culture, artefacts, photos and paintings, including enormous boats and an entire Maori meeting house, sumptuously carved, that you can walk right into. I had tea, bought some cards and then tramped back, down the sleazy Karangahape Road – a long drag of cheap shops, sex parlours, ethnic eateries, trendy music places and so on – before heading back to Vaughan Park on the bus.

(26.v.09)

I was all set to work into the evening, when John rang down and told me there was a Maori group of women staying over, and they were having a cultural evening of song and learning the 'Poi', and I was invited. I've been intrigued by the Poi chant in the New Zealand Prayerbook, so this was a chance to learn more and sit in on a Maori gathering. They were all very warm and welcoming and I soon felt very much part of it; although, like many non-Western cultures, nothing was happening in a hurry, and we spent some two hours after supper learning one Maori song and putting Poi actions to it! Swinging the poi (a little ball on the end of a piece of string) demands some skill and co-ordination, and I wasn't much good at it, but it was fun!

(13.vi.09)

My reading, on this sabbatical, is an untamed, rambling garden, a strange assemblage of books largely garnered from what is available and to hand, and read not systematically, one book at a time, but eclectically, a chapter or two from one book and then something contrasting from another. So currently I am reading David Whyte on work and identity,[68] Philip Pfatteicher on Liturgical Spirituality, Marilynne Robinson's brilliant, eclectic essays When I was a Child I Read Books,[69] an anthology of essays about land and spirituality in Aotearoa New Zealand, and Jenny Pattrick's highly readable novel about the coal-mining settlement of Denniston, a plateau above the south island's west coast, The Denniston Rose,[70] supplemented by an occasional story from Quake Cats, the heart-warming collection of photographs and short stories about cats that survived the Christchurch earthquakes, their exploits and those of their owners[71]....

I'm picking up my earlier fascination with the history, as well as the geography, literature and culture of Aotearoa New Zealand. [When I was here in 2009] I read widely in poetry and took home with me a whole library of New Zealand poetry. I learnt and listened and read of the history of the peoples in this

[68] Whyte, *Crossing the Unknown Sea.*

[69] Marilynne Robinson, *When I was a Child I Read Books* (London: Virago, 2012).

[70] Jenny Pattrick, *The Denniston Rose* (London: Black Swan, 2003). Also *Heart of Coal* (London: Black Swan, 2004).

[71] Craig Bullock, *Quake Cats: Heart-Warming Stories of Christchurch Cats* (Auckland: Random House, 2014).

land, entering many conversations with visitors to Vaughan Park and learning a great deal from conversations with John, Margaret, Joy, Nicky and other staff at VP. I found the model of the Anglican church's three 'tikana' inspiring and instructive as a model of intercultural belonging – even if it has not been wholly successful as a project. I met and listened to the diverse stories and perspectives of Maori and Polynesian Christians, and read works by them, as well as by Pakeha …

Not that there is not an important place for the serious, systematic engagement with the classic texts of a discipline; that is essential for laying the foundations of one's own grounding and creativity. I've spent a good deal of my earlier academic life laying those foundations: all those years at Cambridge reading classic theology texts; then what I've tended to see as the abortive years of my unfinished PhD, but actually they were years in which I read vast amounts on developmental psychology, research methodology, children's religious development, philosophy of religious language and so on; followed by several decades of a varied teaching career in which I've taught – and therefore read up on – everything from New Testament Christology to twentieth century theology, philosophy of language and aesthetics and, of course, feminist theologies and secular feminism as well as practical theology and poetry. So all that is under my belt and gives me the platform upon which to rove freely and eclectically around the limitless range of books and ideas that are available to the curious mind.

If anything, my reading is becoming more and more eclectic and ranging further afield into areas I wouldn't previously have considered. But that stretches the brain and opens the mind, not only to new knowledge, but to think and perceive the world and God's wisdom in it, in new forms; and to acquire fresh language with which to speak of the wonders of creation.

(9.i.15)

Christmas robins

On the way to Milford Sound we stopped to walk in
    woods,
entered a preternatural world of moss and fern and
    stone,
of lichened giants stretching to the sky: a landscape
enclosed, quiet, nothing dramatic to cause comment.
My breathing slowed, I walked reverently, in step.
On the leaf strewn path only inches off, a South Island
    robin
hopped and watched with intent. For all the world
it looked as if he would lead me to the long lost key
that opens the hidden gate, show me the enchanted way
back to the garden where love is naked and newborn.

A year on, and home, I'm making tracks again
to the high walled monastery where I turn
from dizzy winter rush to trudge the ancient paths,
seeking the elusive key. This bright December morning,
after the rising, the singing, the silence, I walk to
St Leonard's Tower. Two red-breasted robins
dart across my path: a warm flash of leafmould and
    firelight.
They eye me before they fly away, reminding me
of winter cheer, hope in hard times, a territory that is
    their own,
a ground where seeds and nuts may be thrown and love
    still grows.

Questions for reflection and prayer

- *What is the conversation you most need to have –*
    - *With yourself?*
    - *With God?*
    - *With another?*
- *Are there conversations you need to unlearn or resist, in order that new conversational space might open up?*
- *Who are the ones you share Sabbath space with? How is Sabbath a social experience for you?*
- *How has God come to you or spoken to you through the stranger or the unexpected encounter?*
- *Which conversations stay with you across time? What were their gifts?*
- *What do you – or might you – learn from animals or birds about Sabbath rest, play, trust and recreation?*

Thoughts
and notes

Chapter 5

Then what is afraid of me comes

The invitation to fear

To live a spiritual life we must first find the courage to enter into the desert of our loneliness and to change it by gentle and persistent efforts into a garden of solitude.

Henri Nouwen[72]

I go among trees and sit still.
All my stirring becomes quiet
around me like circles on water.
My tasks lie in their places
where I left them, asleep like cattle.

[72] Henri J.M. Nouwen, *Reaching Out: The Three Movements of the Spiritual Life* (Glasgow: Fount, 1980): 35.

Sabbath

Then what is afraid of me comes
and lives a while in my sight.
What it fears in me leaves me,
and the fear of me leaves it.
It sings, and I hear its song.

Then what I am afraid of comes.
I live for a while in its sight.
What I fear in it leaves it,
and the fear of it leaves me.
It sings, and I hear its song.

After days of labor,
mute in my consternations,
I hear my song at last,
and I sing it. As we sing,
the day turns, the trees move.

Wendell Berry[73]

Sabbath fear

Perhaps one of the primary reasons we resist Sabbath space – however much we say we want it – is that we are, at some deep level, profoundly afraid of what the encounter with emptiness will bring in its train. If we become truly still, what will we hear in the stillness? If we put down our tasks, lay aside our professional identities and roles, how will we know who we are? If we are willing to enter into emptiness, what if there's nothing there? If we say yes to the wild woods, what if we get lost and never return?

David Whyte, writing about finding our own vocation and claiming our own captaincy, writes of the necessity of

[73] In *This Day*: 7.

facing the 'cliff edge' of our existence, where we confront our greatest fears and, simultaneously, our greatest potency. 'We have to take an inventory not only of the gifts we have to give but of the gifts we are afraid of receiving. What are we afraid of, what stops us from speaking out and claiming the life we want for ourselves? Quite often it is a sudden horrific understanding of the intimate and extremely personal nature of the exploration.'[74]

If we dare take the risk of entering Sabbath space, Berry's poem suggests that we will indeed be confronted by fears, but that these very fears are, at the same time, gifts. The poem's central two stanzas describe an encounter with fear, the allowing of fear to come close and the living in the face of fear, the transformation of fear into gift, and the receiving of the song of the feared thing.

The twofold encounter with fear

There is a twofold encounter with fear, a dual challenge to engage with in this poem. One stanza speaks of 'what is afraid of me' whilst the other of 'what I am afraid of'. For a long time, I puzzled over these two stanzas and couldn't entirely get to grips with them, particularly the first of the two which speaks of 'what is afraid of me'.

Personally, I am much more familiar with the thought that there are things of which I am afraid than that I myself might be a source of fear to others. The poem invites me to reflect on both possibilities. I've spent a good deal of my adult life exploring my own fears, in my writing, in therapy, in feminist groups and with spiritual directors and trusted friends. I've analysed the roots of my fears in childhood, recognized how I've learnt to deal with my fears – in

[74] *Crossing the Unknown Sea*: 54.

more or less functional ways; even been able to manage to transform some of them into positive forces; named them and recognized how my fears are gradually changing. Old ones are no longer the terrifying monsters they were, but new ones have come to take their place.

An inventory of fears

So now, if I ask myself, of what am I afraid, what wakes me in the night to trouble and disturb me, the answer might be something like this. Physical pain, or the prospect of increasing physical pain and incapacity as I get older. In my sixtieth year, I live with and manage a number of minor conditions: rheumatoid arthritis (I hardly notice I have it, it's kept in check by medication), occasional migraines which wipe me out for days at a time (I've had them all my life, but they are getting longer and take longer to recover from and, when acute, are totally debilitating); and perhaps most disruptive when it flares up, the condition of fibromyalgia, a form of muscular pain which can manifest in any area of the body and, when acute, is very painful indeed (a condition which cannot be treated but only managed by strong pain killers or in other ways, such as by exercise, diet and avoiding excessive cold or damp – not easy in the British climate!).

I'm conscious that the level of pain and discomfort I live with is modest compared to others living with chronic and terminal conditions. Nevertheless, pain is a strong reminder of our fragility and mortality, of our dependence on others, and of the uncertainty of our futures. When we are young, unless we have some kind of chronic illness or experience some catastrophe that wounds our body, we tend to take the physical strength and well-being of our bodies for granted, which is part of what gives youth its lithe assurance, beauty and a certain arrogance. With increasing age, the physical confidence of youth is gradually eroded and replaced by a more fragile and knowing resilience. As I enter into my sixties, I begin to have a new awe and respect for all those I know in their eighties and nineties, most of whom live with several conditions they are managing with decreased agility and resources and yet, mostly, with good humour, grace and little complaint. My fear puts me in touch with my fragility, but also helps me to grow an awareness of how increasing physical dependence can bring its own hard-won rewards, as I recognize these in others.

Emotional pain can be as frightening, if not more in some respects, than physical pain, though I am well acquainted with it and, like the migraines, I cannot ever remember a time when it has not been present in my life. I sometimes think it has been part of my vocation to feel the intense emotional pain of my family that other family members can't, or won't, feel. I come from a deeply wounded and broken family (of course, many could say the same), scarred by my parents' broken marriage and broken dreams, the sale of the family farm and the unspoken presence of alcoholism in the family, manifesting as one form of self-medication to dull and drown the pain that is too fearful to face head on. Children of a passionate, deeply-feeling, artistic Celt and a quiet, hard-working, cautious Devonian, my siblings and I have inherited restless, yearning and vulnerable personalities. We each have the capacity for creativity, artistry and generous reaching out towards others, on the one hand whilst, on the other, we can be inclined towards depressive reclusiveness, a strong measure of self-destructiveness and lavish squandering of resources, both financial and otherwise. We manifest various forms of addiction, alcohol being only the most obvious one. Perhaps it is only good fortune and the grace of God that dictated that my particular addictions have been religion and education, both of which have saved me from far more destructive drugs (though of course religion and education also have their less healthy variants and come with potent side effects).

I've had to learn how I've been shaped by my family's heady cocktail of passion, wanderlust, artistry, yearning, silent internalization, passivity, pride and shame, in hurtful and dysfunctional, as well as more healthy ways. At the same time, I've increasingly come to recognize how other members of the family are living out, and repeating, patterns of behavior and relationships that generally lead to victimhood, self-harming and penury. I've had to learn through long and bitter experience that I can do nothing to rescue others from their self-inflicted misery and pain – a role that, as big sister of the family, I tried to fulfill for many years, not only in the immediate family but in many other groups and networks of relationships too. As the oldest girl in the family, I imbibed from birth a strong sense of responsibility for my siblings, but also for my parents. I can never remember a time when I didn't feel responsible for everyone else in the family, when I was not acutely aware of all their moods, feelings, needs, triumphs and failures. I took on the mantle of 'big sister' who looks after everyone else with a vengeance, and found approval and reward in doing so. One of the earliest photos I have shows me, about age five or six, with an arm protectively round my little sister, two years younger than me, and a worried expression on my face.

Rescuing others who situate themselves as victims of circumstances beyond their control – or trying to – is another form of addictive behavior that can dull emotional pain, as well as keep in place the very victim status and mentality the rescuer is attempting to alleviate. Giving up that role of rescuer (or its converse, the persecutor), is a hard work of withdrawal, because it leaves one unprotected from the distress and dysfunctionality over which one now knows oneself to be utterly powerless. So I am afraid of coming too close to my family's pain, because it hurts like hell and, although I am desperate to save them, I know there is nothing I can do to save any of them. Once, I would have waded in, swashbuckler and all. Now, it's all I can do to concentrate on saving myself from all the booby traps and deathly lairs that lie waiting to get me.

I am afraid of my own woundedness and need, of my own capacity to become an alcoholic. I have all the ingredients of an addictive personality, and enough family pain to warrant taking to the bottle. I have to go on the wagon every Lent, simply to demonstrate to myself that I can give up booze for a few weeks without a struggle. The year I can't do it, I know I'm in trouble.

I'm afraid of dying before I've learnt to love my complicated, hurting, needy and dysfunctional family. I'm afraid of failing to live up to my own vision and dreams of myself, of becoming embittered by regret or disappointment for the lives I haven't lived. I'm afraid of the failure of my work; harbouring delusions of genius, I ask myself why I have not become the world famous author I secretly know myself to be, raking in millions and feted by the world's media? Perhaps I'm on the cusp of world domination with the next book, so I'd better keep on writing them.

I'm afraid of growing into my mother (which, of course, I am slowly doing, just as she grew into her own mother – and struggled to accept how alike they were). I'm afraid of growing old and becoming anxious and confused and forgetful and having a house full of worthless clutter and no-one to help me sort it out and look after me. I'm afraid of my body gradually letting me down, causing embarrassment and preventing me doing the things I want or going the places I want to go. I'm afraid of dying alone, abandoned by any who once loved me.

This list of fears is by no means comprehensive. There are many more I could add. Whilst I've concentrated here on my fear of pain, failure, illness, death and abandonment, I spent a good deal of my twenties and thirties being fearful of my own powers, potency, success, creativity and voice – though I only gradually realized it. Many women are, I think, more comfortable with pain and vulnerability – both their own and others – than they are with their own largesse, capacity to act in the world and make a meaningful impact in the public arena, and many of us have had to battle with our own fear of success. My book, *Seeking the Risen Christa,* is an exploration of this theme of overcoming the fear of our own risenness and claiming our risen selves.

Myself as a source of others' fear

Yet exploring our own fears is only one side of the encounter with fear that Berry's poem invites us to address. The other, more startling question, perhaps, is: What or who might be afraid of me? What persons, creatures, states or ideas do I repel through my actions, attitudes or demeanour? Who or what do I hold at arm's length and not allow to come near? This is not a question I've addressed to myself much at all, until challenged to do so by this poem.

A few years ago, the leaving students at Queen's made individually designed and framed 'wordles' for each of the academic members of staff, out of words and phrases the students came up with which they felt named and evoked the particular qualities of each tutor. These gifts are much cherished by all of us, and most of us have them displayed proudly in our studies. Mine includes phrases such as 'lime green feminist' (I have a particularly vivid lime green suit that gets a lot of comment), 'passionate poet', 'lover of cats', 'dangly ear-rings', but amongst the phrases I was intrigued to see (in very small letters, so easily overlooked), 'slightly scary'.

Then what is afraid of me comes

Initially, I was taken aback by this phrase. I do not think of myself as a scary person, yet I have to recognize that I am now a woman in her prime who has claimed her own voice and powers, who has a pretty good idea of what she is about and knows she has limited time left to do all that she wants to do, and who therefore can be fairly direct (and directive!) with others. I do not appreciate wasting time on what does not seem central to my concerns, I can be impatient with others who are slower or more cautious than I am or who simply take my attention away from what I perceive to be my own agenda. My professional status alone gives me a great deal of power (recently increased by becoming a professor), particularly over research students but also over colleagues who are newer to the institution in which I work or have less experience of research and publication. I know I have the capacity to become big, bossy and overbearing (this goes with big sister territory); or perhaps my enthusiasm and quickness to speak simply overrules others or makes them more timid than they otherwise might be. There are, in fact, a hundred ways in which I may be experienced as fearsome by others, and this is something I need to reflect on further and seek to become aware of, in order to guard against being so over-extended in my selfhood that I squeeze out room for others. It is ironic that, having spent half my life struggling to claim my voice and gift, refusing the sins of self-negation and diffuse over-extension which Valerie Saiving Goldstein named as typically female sins in her classic 1960 essay,[75] I now find myself needing to face and resist the more classically male sins of pride, aggression and over aggrandizement of the self!

[75] Valerie Saiving Goldstein, 'The human situation: a feminine view', *The Journal of Religion* 40.2 (1960):100-112.

Intimacy with fear

Whether it is to face our own fears or the fear that others may experience towards us, the encounter in the woods or the wilds necessitates becoming intimate with fear. Very often, when we clear empty space for a quiet day or a retreat, or when we have a more extended period of sabbatical, one of the first things we encounter within ourselves is rising fear, panic, anxiety, even terror. If we are not prepared for this, the dislocation we feel because the experience of space is so contrary to how we may have idealized it beforehand, adds to the sense of panic and anxiety.

This is something I experienced at the beginning of the six-week period of sabbatical I spent at home in 2015, working on the material for this book. What follows is an extended extract from my journal which begins with precisely that sense of dislocation between the beauty of the Maytime and the garden and my own internal state of confusion and terror.

Over time, the fear did ease as I entered into a different way of living – without lists, fixed expectations, hard routines, something I felt strongly drawn to do within my sabbatical. I longed for a different way of living, freed from the normal constraints and routines, and yet putting these habits down (even to not drawing up my habitual 'to do' lists at the beginning of each day!) in order to live a more spontaneous, organically unfolding life, felt incredibly scary. It was truly like entering into the dark, pathless woods without knowing if I'd ever emerge again.

Feeling fear, rather like feeling deep pain, is a deeply uncomfortable experience and one that most of us find ways of keeping at bay – through work, routine, busyness, care of others and so on. Large, unbounded periods of solitude, silence and spaciousness without fixed agenda can allow the habitual safeguards to be loosened, and we then experience our fears in their full force. This is not usually how we have planned or imagined the coveted period of retreat or sabbatical. Yet if we can stay with the reality of whatever feelings may be around; if we can *feel* them, welcome them even, allow ourselves to become intimate with the painful, fearful realities of our internal world, then they may reveal ourselves to ourselves, they may gift us with new insight. Recognising our own fragility and our fear of fear, we can discover the courage to face the fear and to await the unfolding of its gift.

Journal extracts

The garden is gloriously alive with scudding clouds making a patchwork of light and shadow, sudden skits of rain, wind in the chimes and leaves, birds calling and flying. The first roses on Brenda's rambler are intense pink buds, soon to burst – next to the dark blue irises. It's Rosie's birthday, we have had a late breakfast while she opened presents and cards.

And yet my heart is clutched by dread, an unnamable terror.

What is the fear we encounter in sabbatical spaciousness? It is a part of the journey, indeed at its very core, according to Berry's poem that I'm taking as the framework for my exploration of Sabbath – and therefore not to be side-stepped but faced head on, wrestled with, embraced.

When we live our lives at breakneck speed, under the compulsion of relentless pressure (is this how I've come to live my life? Face it – YES!), the sudden gift of spaciousness is terrifying, disorienting. I don't know what to do with it. I'm cast adrift. I long for it, but when it's here I can't seem to grasp it, I don't know how to live it, submit to it.

First of all, I experience depletion. My body wants and needs to go into collapse, lie on the bed for hours staring out the window at clouds and trees. I came across an amazing book on the Brain Pickings website,[76] no longer in print alas – 89 Clouds, a sequence of paintings of clouds by artist Wendy Mark, each one accompanied by a single line of

---

[76] http://www.brainpickings.org

reflection by poet Mark Strand which, cumulatively, make up a long poem.[77] I can totally see the mesmerizing appeal of staring at clouds for hours.

The physical exhaustion echoes an internal depletion, and this is the landscape that terrifies me. My head is empty, my soul is empty, directionless and unable to have pity on itself. Yes, I have all kinds of ideas for projects I 'want' to work on and, indeed, I have begun: sketching out ideas for my essay for the Penny Jamieson festschrift,[78] working in this journal on Sabbath musings, reading this and that. But it feels rather a surface activity. Deep down there's a torpor, a suspension of psychic engagement. I feel like I'm drifting, I'm terrified of wasting this space; and this is because I have such a strong sense of what I 'should' be doing: busily writing, reading, producing something to show for my time. I cannot completely let go into the territory of the wasteland that both draws and terrifies me, so I find myself caught somewhere between meaningful work/activity and complete rest/relaxation. I'm in a limbo land of no-place. Or perhaps this simply is the place I need to be, and it will eventually lead me to the place from which I may be creative. Perhaps this is the place from which I can be creative, though it doesn't feel like it.

Wasteland. Land in which I seem to waste an inordinate amount of time, frittering around the edges of things, coming near, drifting away. What would 'waste' look like?

[77] Wendy Mark & Mark Strand, *89 Clouds* (New York: Aca Galleries, 1999). At https://www.brainpickings.org/2015/03/02/89-clouds-mark-strand-wendy-mark/ Accessed 3.1.19.

[78] Published as 'No Promised Land: A lay theologian reflects on the journey to women's episcopacy in the Church of England', in Jenny Chalmers & Erice Fairbrother (eds.), *Vashti's Banquet: Voices from her feast: Essays to mark the 25th anniversary of the ordination of the first woman diocesan bishop in the Anglican communion: The Rt Revd Penelope Ann Bansall Jamieson* (Council for Anglican Women's Studies, 2015): 174-90.

Sabbath

Getting up late, reading in bed, spending hours writing in my journal, walking up and down the path to the garden noticing things, gazing into the heart of flowers, pulling weeds, hanging out washing, baking bread. Drafting poems. Gathering together fragments of ideas for books, articles, poems.

Why on earth do I consider this 'waste'? Isn't this precisely the life I long to live, here in my garden room, up and down the garden path, hidden away at home where the internal landscape can grow larger, become the place I inhabit, explore? But if this is the life I long to live, why is it so fearful and painful?

Perhaps precisely because I've neglected it so, and now it is hedged about with ambivalence, uncertainty, vulnerability. The path into the woods is dark, foreboding, shadowy from the perspective of the light-filled fields and roads. It takes a while to adjust to the light, to see all the shapes and contours within the woods. It's a totally different landscape in here and you have to find a new way of walking it. Maps won't do. You have to walk by faith, by trust, by instinct, by sense. You can easily get lost. There's a strong compulsion from the rational mind to pull back, retreat, out of the dark and back into light where one can see, where one is still in control. The fearfulness is the terror of losing control, as I feel I am doing in this time. I don't really know what I'm doing here. I haven't even made any lists! – my standard way of proceeding in a day, on a retreat, in a sabbatical period, up to now – as if I'm bone-weary of organizing, plotting, planning, taking responsibility. I spend my whole bloody life looking after everything and everybody, desperately clutching onto an order, a pattern, a list of 'to dos' to accomplish by midnight. I'm sick to the back teeth of it. I want to put down all the lists, burn them. But I don't know how to live without them, I don't know how to find the shape of things if I'm not driven by some outward compulsion, if I don't externalize the internal needs.

Then what is afraid of me comes

Even as I write this, I feel an enormous torpor overwhelming my whole body. I long to put it all down, but I can't. If I were to do that, my fear is I'd totally unravel. I'd collapse and never recover. I'd fall asleep and never re-awaken. I'd go down into the woods and lose myself completely.

And perhaps that's what I need to do. But the prospect is utterly terrifying.

This feels a really scary place to be. Place I haven't visited for a long time. Place inside myself that is anarchic, wild, without boundaries, that resists all control and knows nothing of control. Place that is probably filled with fury, anger, the rage of the untended child. The monster within. The wild witch or bear or ogre deep in the woods, hidden in some cave, that threats to devour/overwhelm, but is actually my own salvation – source of my psychic energy, if I can only face her, face the prospect of being overwhelmed and accede.

(19.v.15)

This is what happens when you go into the woods: all the dark, mangled, tangled parts of your life are waiting there to greet you. We do not dip under the cool ferns and take that beckoning path because we fear to encounter the shadowy creatures of our psyches: the haunted dreams, unhealed memories; the tiny child self who was insufficiently mothered and is crying ceaselessly for the love she will never have enough of; the wounded lover whose failed loves and erotic yearnings are borne as unhealed marks in the flesh, or smarting scars that have healed over but can be knocked/broken open, always vulnerable places in the body; the over-burdened adult self who is so weary, bone-weary, of carrying the ever-increasing weight of all that she has taken upon herself, all that others have loaded on her and she has not resisted, and who is staggering on her knees to get to a clearing by the river where she can put it all down, weep her heart out and sleep for an aeon and a year; the old woman, crone, who is coming towards me bearing enormous amounts of pain and healing in her dried-up, haggard body, a wild look in her eye that I need to gaze into but am afraid of; and behind her, somewhere in a distance I can barely make out, a shadowy, dark-cloaked figure who is my own death waiting for me at the end of all the roads into, and out of, the woods.

No wonder we don't go in there. It is terrifying. It will eat you alive, it will consume the rational, workaday self and spit out the dregs. It has no use for light, mind, rationality, order, control. What use are these in the dark bush? We have to become feral, all instinct, retract thinking from its usual habitation, the mind, and send it to the places it belongs but has retreated from, trained from childhood to distrust: the pores, the senses, the animals' spores that lay a track for the nose to follow.

This is something of what is happening to me, as I enter deeper into the unfettered space of this sabbatical. I have cast off the usual protective layers of my busy, over-planned life. I have not been going out, I have hardly been seeing people, I have been staying here, in my little cabin in the woods. I have found myself very largely incapable of planning this sabbatical, in ways I have done in the past and as I might have expected to do. My mind simply refuses to do it, has shut down on me – in this planning, organizing, controlling mode. I can't even make lists for the day – a habitual means of steering myself through the day, reminding myself of what needs doing and so on. And usually, for any writing project, I have an equivalent 'list': a dedicated notebook with notes on my reading, notes of what yet remains to be read, sketched out structures of chapters, headings, sub-headings and so on. I've not been able to do any of this with this time and project. Another, much more fluid and fearful kind of work has been required of me. The writing in this journal is of a different order: it is an entering into the woods, the places I fear to go. It is a confrontation with my life, and the questions arising from my life as I dare to really attend to it. It is, as David Whyte puts it, an invitation to ask 'beautiful questions',[79] to enter into the conversation with the deepest, truest part of myself. Isn't this precisely what a sabbatical might be for? If not this, what? How did I think it might be otherwise?

Yet 'beautiful' as the questions might be, they are also terrifying – which is why my mind refuses to go there or draws near and then ricochets off, spiraling backwards in retreat. It requires enormous courage, and psychic energy, to confront such questions – which is why, in any given day when I might attempt the conversation (the work of the inner room, the writing life), there might be a couple of hours of intense engagement, and hours of less direct confrontation (reading, note-taking) but also, hours of necessary recovering when I feel as if I'm doing nothing (pottering about the house, tidying things, making bread or cake, weeding or planting in the garden, or simply lying on my bed). It's so easy to feel this is all 'wasted time', even though I know somewhere in my head and my gut it is not. The strong critical parent in me won't lie down and die easily, or for long. 'What the hell do you think you are playing at, woman? What kind of 'work' do you call this, lying in bed til 10.00am, sauntering down to your garden room, writing for a few hours and then stopping? And what kind of writing is this, anyway? Where are your books, or chapters of a book, or articles to show for all this time? And what kind of a book or a chapter or an article is it, anyway? Aren't you supposed

[79] 'The art of asking the beautiful question' is the title of various workshops and retreats given by Whyte. See http://www.davidwhyte.com/events/2018/3/10/a-timeless-way-the-art-practice-of-deepening-any-conversation. Accessed 7.1.19.

to be a serious academic, a 'research scholar', a potential 'professor'? Phaw! What kind of an academic are you? A total phoney!' And so on and so on.

And all of this, of course, is a distraction from the terrifying and beautiful questions I need to be asking myself, the questions that wait for me down in the deep, dark, magical woods. Questions that might look like these:

- Is this what you wish for your life?
- What kind of life is it you most long to be living, and with whom?
- Are you living that life and, if not, why not?
- What is the life, and the work, you have chosen?
- Are you doing the work you were called and made to do, which only you – and no other – can do?
- Are you digging for treasure in the field, and are you willing to give all you have when you find it?
- Are you seeking the pearl of great price or have you scattered your pearls before swine?
- Having recovered that lost coin, swept under the surface of your life, buried away in a dark corner for so long, are you now in danger of losing it again, tossing it out of a carelessly ajar window?
- Have you become the person you are called to be, or someone else?
- Do you like the person you are becoming, the person you live with every day of your life?
- Who are you, anyway? Which of your many selves is sitting in the seat of your life, holding the reins, and is she in the right place?
- How are the different selves – infant, child, adolescent, young woman, mother, parent, adult, wise woman, crone – comporting themselves together, making space for each other (or not)? Are they speaking to, and listening to, each other?

Then what is afraid of me comes

- What violence am I doing to myself and my life by trying to live the life I am living? Whose life is it, anyway? Is it really my life I am living? And if not, whose? And hadn't I better lay this life down and take up my own again?

...What does all this mean? I don't really know, but I have to keep following the way, allowing the questions to form themselves in me and find their own answers.

And then, I simply have to leave off for a while and listen to the rain battering against my garden room windows, watch the tiny May blossom petals spiraling with the raindrops like snow, listen to the birds singing in the rain, look to the trees to tell me how to live with my history, with all the weathers of my internal and external seasons.

(29.v.15)

Into the woods

Come into the woods, she called.
I cannot come yet, I replied,
I must finish my tasks.
I must answer my mother.
I must make myself neat.
I must make myself clever.

Come into the woods, she called.
I may not come yet;
it is dark in there and wet.
There are a thousand insects,
wild animals in the undergrowth,
evil spirits that will undo me.

Come into the woods.
I will not come where
the way is not clear, where
there are no maps, where
the path bends out of sight.
No guide to follow.

Still she calls: *Come into the woods.*
I'm still counting the reasons
for not going, still listening to
my excuses, still looking back
over my shoulder as I duck under cool ferns,
place my feet on the shady path
into the woods.

Questions for reflection and prayer

- *What encounter with fear are you being invited to consent to?*
- *Of whom or what are you afraid?*
- *If you were to make an inventory of your own fears, what would the list include?*
- *What does your fear look or feel or taste or sound like?*
- *What effect does it have upon your life and ministry?*
- *What would it be like to allow this fear to come close and to live a while in its sight?*
- *Who or what might be afraid of you?*
- *What is it in you that might be a cause of fear for others?*
- *What could you do to lay aside that which might be a cause of fear to others in order that they might come close and live for a while in your sight?*
- *Looking back on your life, how have your fears changed, diminished or grown?*
- *Can you recognize and name fears from which you have learnt or received gifts?*
- *What is the conversation you most need to have with your fears?*
- *What 'beautiful questions' might they be posing?*

Thoughts
and notes

Chapter 6

I hear my song ... and I sing it
The recovery of vocation

If we do not come on our own, if we aren't paying attention to our own seasons and the time for return, the Old One will come for us, calling and calling until something in us responds.

Clarissa Pinkola Estés[80]

I go among trees and sit still.
All my stirring becomes quiet
around me like circles on water.
My tasks lie in their places
where I left them, asleep like cattle.

[80] *Women Who Run with the Wolves*: 277.

Then what is afraid of me comes
and lives a while in my sight.
What it fears in me leaves me,
and the fear of me leaves it.
It sings, and I hear its song.

Then what I am afraid of comes.
I live for a while in its sight.
What I fear in it leaves it,
and the fear of it leaves me.
It sings, and I hear its song.

**After days of labor,
mute in my consternations,
I hear my song at last,
and I sing it. As we sing,
the day turns, the trees move.**

Wendell Berry[81]

Being brought back from the state of forgetfulness

At heart, Berry's Sabbath poem is a poem about recovery, remembrance, restoration and transformation. The weary speaker who comes into the clearing in the woods has forgotten who he is, has lost his voice and his song – his vocation and his very identity – through the monotonous stresses and strains of everyday work. 'After days of labor' – the repetition of tasks, of manual work with its demands upon mind and body, of wearying brain work or demanding exchanges with others – the poet is 'mute' in his 'consternations'.

This state of forgetfulness is one we all recognize, I think.

[81] Sabbaths I, 1979, *This Day*: 7.

It is part of the human condition of fallenness – not so much a deliberate accomplishment of evil or a willful turning away from the good (although sin does take such forms, and it is dangerous to pretend otherwise), as a gradual erosion and erasure of what we know to be true, including the truth about ourselves. The pressure of never-to-be-accomplished daily demands, the endless work of 'repairing the world' which is first and foremost God's work, but in which we share, wears away our energy and passion, dulls our senses, desensitizes us from our original, fresh perception and wonder. The demands, but also the rewards, of work, slowly but surely draw us away from the desire that first ignited our sense of vocation.

This may be particularly true of a working life over the long haul. If we remain in one profession or job, we may either lose the 'first love' that drew us to it (if, indeed, love dictated the choice) or, as often happens with promotion and seniority, we may increasingly find ourselves taken further and further away from the very work that we love to do. Teachers, social workers, health care professionals and clergy find themselves promoted into administrative and leadership positions which, paradoxically, remove them from the 'chalk face' or its equivalent. Some thrive on this, and enjoy the challenges; others feel that the spark has gone out of their work and find the responsibilities of seniority burdensome. Success, when it comes, is as dangerous as being barred from the work we long to do. Achievements, titles, awards, recognition – all the things we long for when we don't have them – can very subtly paralyze us from pursuing our work with the passion and drive and single-hearted devotion we might once have brought to it. Promotion and awards can also, of course, sow their seeds of pride, arrogance, entitlement and self-righteousness, which clearly take us away from the sense of our work as gift and grace.

We need Sabbath to step back from the habitual round of absorbing activity in order to bring us back to our senses, to enable us to recover our sense of ourselves: to hear our song and to sing it. The Sabbath space strips and heals us of the layers of accretion that have grown over our perception of ourselves, our sense of vocation, the meaning of our work and our lives. Sabbath clears away the clutter and enables us to see clearly to the heart of who we are and what we are about. Sabbath makes a space in which we may recall and reclaim what we are endlessly prone to forget: that we are not the product of our labours or the sum of our accomplishments, that we do not earn our worth or salvation but that we are graced into being, formed for pleasure, for relationship and for work that is intrinsically meaningful and worthwhile. The meaning of our work lies not first and foremost in what it may accomplish – the outcomes which are the essential drivers of work in most spheres of activity in our contemporary world – but in the rightness of fit for our own God-given graces and talents, the way in which our work expresses who and what we are and what we have been given by God. When there is this rightness of fit, our work reflects and celebrates something of the extraordinary variety, bounty and beauty of creation – and of the Creator. Sabbath reminds us that we are made for joy, for beauty, for glory: to shine out with the particular glory that is ours and ours alone and that will reflect, in a way that no other life can, something of the glory of God.

Being formed by our work — its joys and stresses

Nevertheless, this 'rightness of fit' is not, for most of us, something simply given and enduring without effort, but something we have to work at, reframe and re-forge throughout our working lives. Many of us may have the experience, in the early years of our working lives – if we are blessed to do the work we love to do – of taking to our work like a duck to water, as the saying goes. We are in our element, we flourish and thrive. We swim and move swiftly through the waters, relishing the environment in which we find ourselves, feeling ourselves stretched, stimulated and spent by our work, knowing that we are learning and growing as workers. Our work forms us morally and spiritually into the persons we are. We develop gifts and skills which may have been innate but which only specific practice could hone. Yet we are formed morally and spiritually by our work, as much through its essential challenges and difficulties as by that which gives us ready or easy joy. In one of his Sabbath poems,[82] Berry speaks of 'suffering [himself]/ to be made by days that cannot/ be helped or changed or stopped/', of how he is changed 'by work, by rest', by what he knows into what he knows not.

There are choices we face, often on a daily basis – though we may not recognize it – about where the boundaries of our loyalty and dedication lie: how many hours, over and above our contracted hours, we will give to our work and what the cost (to our families, friends and our own health) of this may be; how far we will comply with the demands of the institution and how far we will resist or challenge them, particularly when they may appear to be unhealthy or even immoral; how we will relate to our colleagues and how much time and energy we will invest in those relationships, as well as the investment we make in the people we are called to serve, whether as pupils, clients, patients or customers, and what the appropriate boundaries of those relationships may be. We make other choices, too: how long we will stay in one job or institution before moving on (if we do), and how we hold in balance the needs of the institution and our own needs or development (which are not always in easy harmony). Sometimes, the choice we would prefer to make is not open to us: we may long to leave our institution, but cannot – for any number of reasons. Or, conversely, we may long to stay, but

[82] Sabbaths IV, 2009, *This Day*: 332.

our short-term contract is not renewed and we are compelled to leave. Then we have to find a way of comporting ourselves that accommodates the disappointment without becoming resentful or bitter, and without simply stagnating as persons.

All of these choices and challenges need somehow to be woven into our sense of vocation, so that the vocation itself is something that does not remain static but grows and changes, perhaps quite radically over a lifetime. In particular, the recovery or renewal of our sense of vocation over time requires the embracing of disappointment and failure – and ultimately, of the ending and erasure of our work and its fruits. We do what we do whole-heartedly, gladly and generously whilst we do it, recognizing its value – a value which is real but partial, temporal in many ways, rather than eternal. Our work lives for a time, as we do, but then passes away, is eroded, buried and forgotten, overtaken and frequently overturned by the person or the generation which succeeds us. One of the hardest challenges of a working life is to leave a job and to witness another person coming into that job and undoing all that we have spent many years building up, cancelling out the fruits of our efforts and bringing an altogether different vision and set of values to the institution in which we worked. Perhaps this is inevitable. Each generation stands on the shoulders of those who came before but strikes out onto new paths not of their elders' choosing or making. We define ourselves in relation to those who came before us, who paved the way for us, and if we do not emulate them (which we sometimes do), we may well break the mould that they set in order to create a new pattern, a new form.

Embracing and integrating failure

Berry's later Sabbath poems explore this theme of embracing and integrating the necessary failure of our work with a clarity and simplicity that is astonishing. He names the failure of his own work with a clear-eyed acceptance, even a kind of joy, which I find extraordinary and highly challenging. Thus, in one of the 2007 Sabbath poems, he walks by a field where he had, in the past, cultivated crops. It is now returned to woods, reclaimed by the forest.

> And I think of all the effort
> I have wasted and all the time,
> and of how much joy I took
> in that failed work and how much
> it taught me.[83]

In a number of other poems, he envisages the undoing of his life's work, the return of the cultivated fields to forest, the falling into ruin of every built house and habitation, the erasure of all texts and words, even. Beyond acceptance, there is a glorious exultation in what he describes, thrillingly, as the 'resurrection of the wild', 'the second coming of the trees.'[84] In a kind of reversal of the prophetic vision of Isaiah 35, in which the wilderness is turned into a cultivated garden, Berry envisages the triumph of the wilderness over humanity's attempts to tame and civilize it, the uprising of the forests which once, of course, covered the entire planet. A similar vision of the triumph of the trees is envisaged by Ali Shaw in his imaginative fantasy novel, *The Trees*, in which the forests re-assert themselves and lay claim to the towns and cities of England[85] – a dystopian unfolding which the human characters in the novel respond to variously as unprecedented disaster or as the only kind of salvation possible in the world. As a metaphor within which to consider our own lives, including the significance of our work, such a vision of the wild reasserting its claim

[83] Sabbaths 2007, IX, *This Day*: 309.
[84] 'Window poems', no 12. In *New Collected Poems*: 93-4.
[85] Ali Shaw, *The Trees* (London: Bloomsbury, 2016).

on reality speaks to us of the end of all human framing, categorizing and plotting. It puts one's own little human life, endeavours and projects into true perspective: a tiny thing, not necessarily mean or insignificant in itself, but a little thing, a thing of the earth, a fragment of the whole that will pass away soon enough and be absorbed back into the whole, re-composted into the soil from which we came.

'How much joy I took in that failed work', says Berry. This is an extraordinary thing to be able to say, and I am not sure that I can say this yet of my own work . I am still all too attached to its success, rather than being ready to embrace its failure and demise. Yet, as I reflect further on Berry's words I recognize that, looking back on my life, I can claim the value of apparently wasted work at an earlier stage of my career, although I may not be able truthfully (yet) to say 'how much joy I took in that failed work'.

For many years in my twenties and early thirties, I struggled to write a PhD thesis and, in fact, never completed that first PhD (I went on to start a new PhD in my late thirties and successfully completed it). Looking back, I realize I should never have embarked on a PhD straight after finishing my first degree (something that is less common these days but at that time, was quite routine in Cambridge). I had very little idea of what undertaking research entailed; I hadn't even written an undergraduate dissertation, let alone a Masters level piece of research. I was encouraged by some of my teachers and mentors to embark on research and I suppose I did so in a naïve fashion, without really considering what the life of a PhD student was like or counting the cost. No one advising me thought to help me imagine the reality of what doing research might actually look like in practice, and at that time there was very little training or support beyond the infrequent meetings with one's supervisor (and I went through a succession of badly-chosen supervisors).

Having floated into doctoral studies, and acquired

funding for three years full-time study, I spent those three years in a state of more or less perpetual confusion and deep unhappiness, not really knowing what I should be doing and gradually losing my academic confidence as I failed to progress the work and bring it to a satisfactory conclusion. For the first time in my life, I found academic study difficult. Up until that point, I had sailed through school and my first degree, working hard but finding the work satisfying and full of joy, achieving top marks without having to do more than what came naturally to me. Now, for all the hours and hours I spent reading and writing and trying to draft chapters, I had no real self-belief or confidence in what I was doing and knew, in my heart, that it wasn't working. I was deeply miserable and I wasn't going to be able to finish it. Yet somehow, I couldn't face that truth and make the honourable decision to withdraw. I had set myself to do it, I had received funding to do it. And then I got a job on the basis of the unfinished PhD, which made it even harder to think of giving it up. And so I continued to try to finish it, spending years on research that never materialized into a completed thesis – even though I did publish a handful of articles and, in that sense, I suppose, the work was not wholly wasted.

But I experienced a profound sense of failure over the uncompleted PhD and, with it, a deep and pervasive shame. This was a long and painful experience of paralysis and the root of it, I later came to see, was a fear of success and a fear of claiming my own power in the world – a theme I have explored elsewhere.[86] The point here is that, much later on, I have come to see the value and the profound ways in which this experience of failure has shaped me, for good rather than for evil, and therefore I now embrace the failure as an essential part of who I am and who I have become through that failure. At the time – and this was a long period, a good decade of my life

---

[86] *Seeking the Risen Christa* (SPCK, 2011).

– I was paralyzed and stuck in the realization of my vocation and this was a deeply frightening and undermining thing. I was lost, floundering in the dark. I knew I wanted to be a writer, I was called to be a writer, yet this experience of academic failure almost destroyed my ability to write. I lost my voice and my sense of who I was. And yet, out of this experience of profound failure, I learnt to be a more compassionate teacher (and, I hope, human being) than I ever could have been without those years of wrestling and failed work. For of course, many students and perhaps most doctoral students (the main category of student I am working with), struggle with precisely this challenge of finding their own voice, having confidence in their own capacities and forging a meaningful piece of work that can stand within the public arena and withstand the critical scrutiny of academics and peers. Had I not undergone those long and painful years of wrestling with my own failed work, I do not think I could accompany others who wrestle with their own sense of inadequacy and failure, as I have been taught to do through my own failure. Whilst I cannot (yet) say that I took joy from the failed work, I can say, with Berry, 'how much it has taught me.'

Through the failure of his work and the reclamation of cultivated fields by the forest, Berry learns to foresee and welcome his own demise. 'In time', he reflects, 'a man disappears/from his lifelong fields', and goes on to speak of foreseeing such a future 'with hope,/ with thanks.'[87] The poem ends, 'Let others come'. It is only as we disappear from our own fields – whatever, for us, those fields might be – that we make room for the next generation to come. This is a conviction Christians should be utterly at home with, given the centrality of the paschal cycle to our faith, with its teaching of the necessary death of the seed in the soil in order that new life can emerge. Yet many of us – myself included –

---

[87] Sabbaths, 2007, VII, *This Day*: 307.

struggle to let go our firm grip on our work and its products, and do not share Berry's deep faith in the ecology of nature, the cycle through which the death and waste product of one form becomes the seedbed and manure of the next.

The gift of seeing our work afresh

The regular, rhythmic stepping back of Sabbath is essential for us to gain some kind of true and lasting perspective on our work, to recognize its real worth – including the worth of what must, ultimately, fail and return to dust. Whilst we labour in the fields (for which, read 'classroom, studio, factory, hospital, board room, kitchen, law court' or whatever), we are too immersed in the immediacy of our labour to be able to assess its real worth. It is only as we step back, for longer or shorter periods of time, that we can begin to see from a wider vantage point and, seeing, judge clearly the worth of our work and the ways in which it is shaping and changing us. In the light of such clarity, we are enabled to make fresh choices about whether and how to re-engage when we return to the fields.

This is one of the gifts of a longer period of sabbatical when we remove ourselves for several months from our working environment, or at the very least lay aside the normal tasks of our working life (I recognize that not everyone can or chooses to move right away from their context of work, although I consider it much harder to reap the fruits of a sabbatical if one remains in one's own work context). Although a sabbatical may entail a commitment to a specific piece of work (study, writing, travel and so on), and we may find much satisfaction and refreshment in being able to achieve the goals we set ourselves, the deeper gift of sabbatical space is generally something else, some wider gift or blessing we did not expect or look for. The space away from our routine tasks and environment enables healing or restoration of something lost, abandoned, given up for dead; a renewal of vision or purpose; a new way of seeing or experiencing one's life, one's work, one's home, one's place and calling in the world.

I would certainly say this was true of my three month sabbatical at Vaughan Park in New Zealand, in 2009. I arrived depleted, exhausted, ill, my body and soul wrung out with the ravages of work and life. I settled down to do my work, in the rhythm of the days. I read, I slept, I prayed, I ate, I walked the beach. I worked on my book, I wrote poems. But more than this, I fell in love with the place and the people around me. I felt strangely at home in the landscape of Aotearoa New Zealand. I learnt about the history and cultures of its peoples, and the inextricable links with my own homeland and history. I read and heard New Zealand poetry and acquired my own little library of native poets. The landscape, flora and fauna offered me new imagery and metaphors for the spiritual life, a new language for praying, and I wrote a sequence of Aotearoa Collects based on my response to the new topography.

Perhaps the greatest gift was the perspective on my own context provided by the distance of being somewhere completely different, immersing in the new culture and setting, alongside the freedom from my usual roles and tasks. This is a paradox much attested by travelers: that it is only by leaving home and going away to some distant clime and country that we begin to recognize where we truly belong and who we really are. The unfamiliar cleanses our over-familiarised perceptions, rinses the lazy eye clean of its habitual images, shocks the senses into seeing what was tired and old in fresh, new ways, from the enlarging perspective of distance. It was only in coming to New Zealand that I saw and recognized various features of my UK context that would be blindingly obvious to a Kiwi but that I had never really noticed before.

The relative isolation of New Zealand from other nearby countries and its small population, with less developed specialisms than in the UK, caused me to appreciate, as I had not done before, the accessibility of an enormous range of opportunities and choices in my own context. How easy it is for those of us with the means to travel around Europe and even to other parts of the globe (far more expensive to those from the Antipodes) to take this accessibility of other places and peoples and their cultures for granted. The sheer size of Europe and the range of professional specialization in most spheres offers job opportunities that are simply impossible in other parts of the world. And of course, anyone from the 'old world' who visits a country with a much more recent history, tends to appreciate in a new way the extraordinary historical treasures of their own, long inhabited land. I began to miss and yearn for ancient buildings, streets and churches, appreciating the rootedness and longevity of my own British context, including a faith which is earthed in a centuries old heritage. (Of course, that heritage is complex and marked by much that is evil – colonialism and slavery being the more glaring examples – as well as much that is good. Learning more about New Zealand's experience of colonization and the suffering of Maori and Polynesian peoples also afforded me opportunity to reflect upon the experience of those on the underside of British history.)

On a more personal level, I came to Vaughan Park at a particular juncture in my professional life where I thought I had exhausted the trajectory I had been travelling. I fully expected the sabbatical to mark the beginning of the end of my time at Queen's, providing the impetus to look for a new job and make my move. Instead, I found a new perspective on my working life at Queen's, a new way of thinking about my work altogether, a way of knitting life and work into a more integrated, organic whole – and this enabled me to return to my work and 'know it for the first time', as Eliot's famous phrase has it.[88] Nearly ten years later, I can look back and see how my professional life has flourished and developed since 2009, taking off in a new direction in a way that has almost been like starting a new job, only without the inconvenience of having to move somewhere else! I have taken up a new leadership role within the institution and gone full-time over the past few years, and in the last couple of years have been made professor at our partner university in Amsterdam: something I could not possibly have anticipated when I set out on my sabbatical in 2009. I suspect I am far from unique in this. Those fortunate enough to have been granted a sabbatical from their work could tell stories about how the sabbatical experience renewed their sense of vocation or gave them the clarity and courage to go in a new direction, take a major decision or take up a new challenge.

Hearing our song and singing it

Berry's poem offers the metaphor of finding a voice, a song, as an image which expresses the discovery – or recovery – of our own vocation. This is a powerful metaphor which has been employed, in particular, by feminists over the past several decades as an image of women coming into their own, claiming their identity and power, and speaking out from the patriarchal silence which denied them a voice. The poem moves, as it develops, from muteness to song, from listening to uttering, and this can represent the rhythm of silence and speaking, of receiving and giving, which is at the heart of the Sabbatical rhythm of rest and work. It may also capture something of the journey from powerlessness to agency, from invisibility to visibility, from lostness to home-

[88] T. S. Eliot, 'Little Gidding, V', in *Four Quartets*. Freely quoted throughout the web, for instance at https://www.huffingtonpost.com/2013/09/26/ts-eliot-quotes_n_3996010.html?guccounter=1 Accessed 3.1.19.

coming, which many feminists and others have charted as the journey to be undertaken by all who seek to claim their authentic selfhood and their rightful place in the world.

When we come to our senses, hear our song and sing it – when we claim our unique selfhood and vocation and live it – we find that our place in the order of things is restored. 'The day turns, the trees move'. The poem ends on an apparently unspectacular, utterly ordinary note. We come back to ordinariness, to dailiness, to the rhythm of things; as we must. The withdrawal of Sabbath is followed by the re-engagement with the world of work. Work is born out of rest and leads back into rest once again; and rest enables a fresh appreciation and perception of our working lives. The poet returns to the everyday world of the turning days and the moving trees, and knows himself to be a part of this natural rhythm and harmony, not apart from it. Healed by the very trees, the poet attends to these trees as things in themselves, notices their movement in a way he did not at the start of the poem. His rest has given birth to a new attentiveness, a new harmony.

Notice that the poem ends with the 'I' of the speaker changing into a collective 'we'. The 'I' who has been the subject of the poem all the way through until now – 'I go among trees and sit still' – merges quietly with the 'we' of those who sing: 'As we sing/ the day turns, the trees move'. Who is this collective 'we'? I think Berry is imagining here the song of the birds, which we have encountered in stanzas two and three, now being joined by the song of the human. Having sat in stillness in the circle of trees and allowed the creatures of the wild to emerge and come close, having received their gifts and listened to the song of the birds, the man at last hears his own song and sings it, joining in the symphony of the birds. In its utter simplicity, the end of the poem indicates the restoration of the natural order of which human beings, in their working and their resting, are a part.

Journal extract

Back to Berry's Sabbath poems – their pure, astringent taste in the parched throat. A whole draught of them this morning after the hour and a half in chapel (morning prayer, silent prayer, eucharist), after breakfast (the slow delicious physical feeding in the silent refectory following the spiritual feeding). I haven't been reading them enough; whole days have gone by when I haven't managed morning prayer, such is the crazy demand of work; or, if I have managed it, the office has been brief, my morning poem snatched out of time's fierce glove, and the words have not gone deep in me. But now it is time, if late, to 'begin again', as Berry says, in order that I may, 'save [my]self, heartwhole'[89] (what an arresting, beautiful image).

There is a return, as Berry well knows, again and again, to the root, to the land, to 'the waters of origin',[90] from which we endlessly depart to our world-wearying work. Work that has become, to many of us, our chief burden, our torment, our daily endurance and suffering (how on earth did this happen? And especially how did and can it happen in the sacred assembly of the church where work should be to the glory of God and our own dignity and growth in wisdom, rather than the fearsome assault on mind and body it so often seems?).

To return to the source requires intent, persistent courage and, as Berry puts it in this poem, a kind of wading or swimming upstream, against the current that would, without

[89] Sabbaths, ll, 2007, *This Day*: 299-300.
[90] Sabbaths, ll, 2007, *This Day*: 299.

our resistance, carry us headlong over the roaring cataract, plunge us to our death. The insidiousness of work, as machine, as relentless pressure – especially when it is essentially good and meaningful, 'for the sake of the kingdom'. It is never accomplished, there is always more of it, it is a hungry beast. The more we feed it, the hungrier it becomes and the more insistent its demands. The working days grow longer and longer, the mind and body speed up to try and keep up, I find myself rushing through the day, at war with my body, in the vain pursuit of efficiency. The most precious parts of the day – prayer, silence, exercise, relaxation, leisurely meals with Rosie – get squeezed out, or pared down to a minimum.

Against this madness I must not struggle or protest or prevaricate, but simply stop. Turn around, walk away – stone by stone, coming slowly up the monastery track – a journey that simply cannot be hurried, the ruts and pits won't allow it – till I get back to where I started: the source, the origin, the 'heartwhole' place of repair.

Sabbath is, itself, just such a return to origins: a rhythm for righting what has become out of shape or out of true, a return to blessed rest and order, the equilibrium in which things can assume their proper shape, come to rest and, at rest, become poised for movement again. Sabbath is a return to God's original intention for the creation – blessing and generativity. Sabbath is a repeated, weekly remembering: 'remember the Sabbath day, and keep it holy' (Exodus 20:8): a reorientation to our source and ground of being, God; a turning aside from all our labours and efforts in order to rediscover the gift of our own existence, the sheer mystery and beauty of life – our life, my life – held in being and sustained by grace.

In keeping Sabbath, we 'remember that the world in which we live has been created by God and that we ourselves have been created "in the image of God". Our bodies move to a rhythm of work and rest that follows the rhythm originally strummed by God on the waters of creation. As God worked, so shall we; as God rested, so shall we. Working and resting, we who are human are in the image of God. At the same time, remembering the holiness of the day also reminds us that we are not God: this is a commandment, not a polite invitation. Though we are made to do good work and to enjoy consecrated rest, we can be the makers of neither commandments nor days. These we receive.[91]

After work, rest. All I want to do is sleep, now that I'm here and everything begins to drop away. I lay on my bed for an hour this morning and had to drag myself up at 11.00am, half drugged. After dinner, I went out for a walk – not my usual brisk pace, too tired for that – taking it very slowly and paying attention to the autumnal woods, the gorgeous golden light, the cloud-flecked skies. Holly bushes/trees thick with berries, gleaming and glistening against the dark leaves. By the time I walked back up the monastery track, I was ready for another lie-down before tea and chocolate cake (brought by a visiting interfaith group).

Now the light begins to fade, colours muted outside my big picture window. The huge grey sky will grow darker and darker, gradually stripping all light and colour from the scene. The dark is an invitation to rest, to sleep, to give up all striving.

> Heart's ease
> Body's release
> Soul peace

(28.x.15)

[91] Dorothy C Bass, *Receiving the Day: Christian Practices for Opening the Gift of Time* (San Francisco: Jossey-Bass, 2000):47-8.

Return

There is an ocean I am always returning to
travelling halfway round the world
to come home to its long bay

I walk along the edges of surf
searching for greenstone and pāua shell
feel the grit under my feet

taste the tang of salt in my mouth
rinse my mind's eye clean

I want to trudge as far as the tide will sing to me
slapping bare feet on sand in time with the sea's fret and fray
walk out of my weariness and forgetfulness

stay as long as the waves come and go
til the moon rises and stars appear in the southern sky the
ocean gathering darkness, slipping me over its long
    white cloud[92]

[92] Originally published in *NZ Books,* June 6, 2018 (28.2): 26.

Questions for reflection and prayer

- *What are you most in danger of forgetting about your vocation and calling? How can you remind yourself?*
- *How has your vocation – or your sense of calling – changed over the years?*
- *How has your living out of your vocation continued to form and shape you, morally and spiritually?*
- *Are you in danger of losing touch with the 'holy fire' that has been lit within you? How can you 'still stir up' that fire within?*[93]
- *What have you learnt from failure in your life and ministry?*
- *As you contemplate your eventual retirement and death, how do you feel? Can you rejoice in the failure and erasure of your work, as Berry's poems do? Or do you rage against the dying of the light, as Dylan Thomas's famous poem has it?*
- *How might you practise more faithfully the rhythm of Sabbath in your life and ministry? Does the relation between 'woods' and 'fields' – withdrawal and engagement, rest and work – need to be rethought or reworked?*
- *Where do you see opportunities for stepping back or aside, pausing or resting in the course of work, letting go – within the effort and the labour?*

93 The reference is to Charles Wesley's hymn, 'O Thou who camest from above', particularly to verse 3 and the line, 'Still let me guard the holy fire'.

Thoughts
and notes

Chapter 7

The day turns, the trees move

Coming out of the woods

I go among trees and sit still.
All my stirring becomes quiet
around me like circles on water.
My tasks lie in their places
where I left them, asleep like cattle.

Then what is afraid of me comes
and lives a while in my sight.
What it fears in me leaves me,
and the fear of me leaves it.
It sings, and I hear its song.

Then what I am afraid of comes.
I live for a while in its sight.
What I fear in it leaves it,
and the fear of it leaves me.
It sings, and I hear its song.

After days of labor,
mute in my consternations,
I hear my song at last,
and I sing it. **As we sing,
the day turns, the trees move.**

Wendell Berry[94]

The return from Sabbath

For most of us, of course, it is not possible to stay in the woods permanently (unless we are woodcutters or hermits – and even they come out from time to time). Wendell Berry speaks of the tension in which most of us live out our lives most of the time between the solitude and renewal of the woods and the engagement with others and our work in the field (his image for the human world of work), in a beautiful little reflection – half essay, half extended prose poem – entitled 'Healing.'[95] It is a reflection on the meaning and value of our work and how good work is intrinsically connected to solitude and rest. In it, he speaks of the 'true solitude' that is found in the wild places, where one is 'without human obligation'. In such a place, or state, 'one's inner voices become audible' and, 'in consequence, one responds more clearly to other lives'. Yet one cannot remain

[94] Sabbaths I, 1979, *This Day*: 7.
[95] Wendell Berry, 'Healing', in *What Are People For?* (Berkeley: Counterpoint, 2010): 9-13.

perpetually in that solitude of the wild place: there is no escaping the return:

> From the order of nature we return to the order – and the disorder – of humanity.

> From the larger circle we must go back to the smaller, the smaller within the larger and dependent on it…

> And having returned from the woods, we remember with regret its restfulness. For all creatures there are in place, hence at rest…

> In the circle of the human we are weary with striving, and are without rest.[96]

A few months after returning from sabbatical and the Scholars' gathering, I certainly resonated with Berry's description! I returned with high ideals and plenty of resolutions to keep the spaciousness of my time away at the centre of my working life: to a large degree I have failed, and probably had to fail. There is no escaping the return to the work of the field (or, in my case, the classroom, the study, the kitchen, the meeting room, the chapel). The good thing about going away is going away: the hard thing is coming back! Not that I wasn't ready to come home, and be re-united with my partner and the cats and our home and garden (ordinary and imperfect as they all are). Re-entry at work was another matter. I was more or less immediately submerged in a backlog of two months' worth of emails, student work to read, supervisions to catch up on, colleagues to re-engage with, student crises to respond to, teaching, planning and administration (and so on and so on), from which I've never

[96] Berry, 'Healing':11-12.

really emerged (only to be saved from the pressures by my next, looming sabbatical!). More problematically, I was immediately re-immersed in a working culture that seems to me disordered: endlessly driven, restlessly striving and with very little sense of boundary or respect for the body (and I mean here both the physical body of the individual and the body ecclesial and politic of the community). Both church and academic cultures in the UK (and perhaps elsewhere too) seem to be captive to a relentless drive to achieve and to produce, in defiance of the depletion of resources both financial and human; and the institution for which I work is embedded in both cultures, captive to their demands. My challenge, shared with my colleagues, is how to survive in this environment without capitulating to the culture, how to maintain a vision of a different way to live and work – the kind of way of which Berry and others such as David Whyte write.

Yet, if I haven't managed to keep the degree of spaciousness and solitude at the heart of my work as I might have liked, I know I'm in a very different place from where I was before I went away – and this itself testifies to the value of Sabbath and sabbatical. I am physically rested and healthier; I am replenished in my soul and affections and mind; I have a mind and memory stocked with images of beauty and places to which I may return at a moment's notice; I am enriched by new friendships as well as old ones, and know myself to be supported and encouraged by those I met on my travels whose care reminds me that I am not a machine and that I owe it to myself, as well as to them (not to speak of God) to care for myself. All these things have enabled me to submit to the necessary immersion without fear or panic, in a steadiness of spirit and with a measure of hope, even a certain joy, that would not have been possible without the sabbatical. I've accepted my own limitations more patiently, doing what I can each day and leaving the rest to wait for another day. I often use that lovely prayer from Night Prayer in the New Zealand Prayer Book:

> It is night after a long day.
> What has been done has been done;
> what has not been done has not been done;
> let it be. [97]

Every night, there is the opportunity to practise relinquishment of control and trust of our waking lives, with their work and endeavours, into God's hands, as we enter into the not-being, not-doing, receptive state of sleep. Every night, there is an opportunity to receive again the renewing, nourishing gifts of sleep: the nightly Sabbath of the unconscious which sustains the rest of our waking, daily life and reminds us of how so much of our life is hidden, mysterious, unknowable by us – including that which most nourishes and sustains us.

A right ordering of things

Within this daily pattern of work and rest, sleep and consciousness, Berry speaks of a certain 'order' in our work which 'is the only possibility of rest'.[98] This order has little to do with good organisation or techniques for keeping on top of your emails (though these things may be helpful in themselves). Rather it is a more profound spiritual and theological 'order', a right ordering of things, in which the connection between the woods and the fields is maintained; that is, in which we keep a strong memory of the wild places

[97] 'Lord, it is night', Night Prayer, The Anglican Church in Aotearoa, New Zealand and Polynesia, *A New Zealand Prayer Book* (HarperCollins, 1997):184.
[98] Berry, 'Healing':12.

of rest, solitude and replenishing alive in our striving and endeavours in the place of work and return to them for interludes whenever we can. This right order also resides in a certain humility which resists both pride and despair – closely related bedfellows. For both pride and despair are rooted in a sense that our well-being, and that of others in our care, depend entirely on our own efforts and that therefore we may never lift our hands from our work. As Berry puts it:

> One is afraid that there will be no rest until the work is finished and the house is in order, the farm is in order, the town is in order, and all loved ones are well.

By stating it in this way, we recognize how illusory is the fantasy that often drives our work. The work will never be finished, the house and the farm and the town will never be in order and our loved ones will never be wholly well – not all of them, all of the time. Yet to recognize this is not to fall into despair or to deny the dignity and significance of our daily toil, which is offered as an expression of our love and care for our house, our farm, our town and our loved ones. We offer what we can and then lay the pen or the spade or the ladle down when we have come to the end of the day (or the working week).

> Let tomorrow come tomorrow. Not by your will is the house carried through the night.[99]

We are not alone

Nor are we alone in our labours – another illusion that we can cherish, as if the house and the town depend entirely

[99] Berry, 'Healing': 13.

on our efforts, and our efforts alone. This is the hubris or pride that destroys both our own peace of mind and the well-being of others, paradoxically – even while we delude ourselves that we are motivated entirely by a care for them. No, against the 'pride of thinking oneself without teachers', Berry asserts: "The teachers are everywhere. What is wanted is a learner."[100]

Who are our teachers? Berry does not spell it out, but I think he has in mind more than human teachers, though there are certainly plenty of those, and he speaks of 'the love and the work of friends and lovers' which 'belong to the task, and are its health'. We know how the love and friendship of colleagues, as well as friends and lovers, helps to sustain us in the task and to enliven the work with joy and humour. Their work joins hands with our work, and in collaboration we may do so much more than is possible alone. It is not simply that the work is divided and shared out, but that the company of colleagues and friends transforms the work. We work in and out of community, and the community both sustains and shares the work.

Yet this community is not simply a human one, and I think Berry has in mind teachers other than the human. The woods themselves may be our teachers, as they have certainly been Berry's over many decades, with the creatures that live there; to which we should also add the skies and the rivers and the seas – the natural world which, however much we exploit and deplete it, continues in its cycles of rest and renewal, its seasons of growth, expansion and decay. As we learn from them, so we come to understand that 'rest and rejoicing belong to the task, and are its health'.[101]

[100] Berry, 'Healing': 13.
[101] Berry, 'Healing': 13.

Journal entries

At the monastery it is a grey, wet day, my window filled with the branches of the apple tree but a dull grey-white sky beyond rather than the blue dazzle of yesterday. I don't want to leave. I'm only just arriving, settling into the silence. I crave more of this life-giving draught. I need to come back soon (find a time in the diary). But I'm still here, I haven't left yet! I have all of this lovely, empty day to be here, steeped in silence.

I am reading Wendell Berry's Sabbath poems – a great collection of several hundred of them from 1979 to 2013 – taking this as my daily meditation text for Lent. Such stunning poems; and each one, an invitation into the stillness and the beauty of Sabbath space. Every day, I may return to the woods and find blessed sustenance to resource me for the work of the 'fields' – or, in my case, the study, the classroom, the staff room.

The seventh poem in the 1979 sequence addresses directly my dilemma of how to return to working days and maintain the vision of the Sabbath, recognizing the pain and grief of that work-a-day world yet also offering hope that 'work day/and Sabbath [may] live together in one place', thereby generating a harmony, 'though mortal, incomplete', that 'is our one possibility of peace.' [102]

There is such wisdom and hope in this poem, a teaching I need to indwell and recite and learn deeply – take its hope

[102] Sabbaths VII, 1979, *This Day*: 16.

with me into my working days. Berry knows 'it is a hard return from Sabbath rest', naming 'the grief of waste, the agony of haste and noise'[103] – and what relief and balm even to have this named! That haste and noise are both 'agony', a kind of physical and spiritual pain that marks out a world of work in which there is simply too much to do and insufficient time in which to do it so that one cannot work in the slow, patient, contemplative manner and pace that one's heart longs to settle into. And not only must one 'haste' through the relentless pressure of tasks, but one must work in an environment of noise: constant chatter, busy, wordy worship, meals in a dining room ringing with din, meetings and classes where talk barely pauses – and in buildings designed for functionality, with little or no aesthetic value, no space for the soul to breathe – even if we weren't spilling out of the rooms, desperate for more space.[104]

Yet, though the poem names this 'agony', it nevertheless goes right on to 'rejoice' in the 'returning', speaking of 'being blessed' in the vision that has been given in the Sabbath space – a 'vision of what human work can make'. Though hard labour, human work is also seen as graced and blessed by God, partaking of the 'harmony between the forest and field' (the wild and cultivated, the natural and the human orders), the creative realization of the world as it was intended to be, 'given for love's sake', 'by love and loving work revealed'. [105]

How is it possible for work to be 'loving' when it is situated within the 'agony' of haste and noise', 'the grief of waste'? (Of course, I'm aware of writing this as an introvert

---

[103] Sabbaths VII, 1979, *This Day*: 16.
[104] Since writing this, Queen's has been able to expand with a new, purpose-built residential and learning space, Frances Young House, which has alleviated a good deal of the pressure on space experienced in the period in which I was writing.
[105] Sabbaths VII, 1979, *This Day*: 16.

who craves silence and solitude for my best work; there are other colleagues, out and out extraverts, who probably love the din and endless busyness of our work environment!) It is able to be loving because it looks beyond the waste, the haste and the noise, to the 'gift that nurtures and protects': the endless outpouring of life and time from the hand of God, the original vision of fecundity and harmony that marks the creation and which human beings are called, with God, to work to restore. 'When field and woods agree', when mortal and natural orders work together for the common good, the 'first Sabbath's song' is evoked and recalled, its music arriving on our ears as from heaven, both 'promise' and 'prayer'. Yet it is 'an earthly music', a music that we may make out of our work – when done in tune with God's – and in that music find rest and hope again.

(19.ii.15)

And now it's time to go – I'm sitting at the station, fifteen minutes early, and I'm leaving reluctantly, leaving half my heart at the abbey[106] – even though I'm also glad to be going home, to practise living humanely, gently, with as much Benedictine balance as I can manage. I have a whole week at home on my own ... and, though there seem to be more meetings with people than I had really hoped and intended, there is plenty of space and time around them. And, having given my heart and body what they most desire here – blessed silence, the beauty of the offices, the bareness and unclutteredness of the place, its simplicity and order, rest, exercise for the body, an interlude for the exhausted self to recover itself, remember its roots and rediscover the interior well – having given, been given, so much, I don't feel so resentful of all the people who seem to be clamouring at

[106] Malling Abbey, West Malling

my life, asking for something (attention, time, care, love, respect). I might have something to give them; I might even receive something, dear heart!

Burdened and over-committed as I generally am, I very easily come to resent others, regard them as so many distractions from my 'real' work and vocation – God forgive me! – rather than an essential part of my life and a gift from God to me. I'm so blessed to have so many people in my life who love me, need me, want me, wish to share much that is good with me; how many people in the world are desperate for such companionship?

(24.vii.11)

So now I'm home again, and the challenge and opportunity is to love my own life here, at home; to love and cherish ordinariness, the mundane, the unspectacular as the place where I may practise holiness. It's here, not the monastery, where I am called to pray, to work, to eat, to live, to love, to praise. It's here where I'm given an opportunity to create a rhythm, a gentle balance, a structure that can hold everything together before God.

(25.vii.11)

Faithfulness

Work the same patch every season.
Come to know a place in all its guises:
sleeping in shadow, blazing in sunlight.
Love the plant in winter, when it says nothing:
watch the leaves fall, sink back into mould.
Cut your losses, let the past go, pitch into dailiness.
Every morning, rise at the same hour,
splash water over face and body,
dress in silence. Give the self to prayer,
repeat the formulas, breathe newness into them.
Guard the doorways of dawn, dusk, nightfall:
liminal spaces where promises can be made again,
faithlessness forgiven.
                              Long, routine hours of daylight
pledged to the ordinary: baking bread others will eat,
repairing fabric others will wear. Keep the tools
of your trade supple, oiled. Handle them carefully.
Pick up the pen or ladle with gentleness, return to the
same page and hungers without impatience or despair.

The days come and go. Nights shorten.
Cold rises to its apex, crushes
the memory of summer. The moon
makes her journey. Autumn comes round
again: the trees are ready to let go. Always,
this fall and rise: the rhythm of breathing,
of ebb and flow. Let us forgo

the distraction of elsewhere: valleys
we might have wandered in but didn't, roads
that would have taken us some place we'll never now
discover. As the years and the days lengthen,
the unforsaken hearth offers its unfashionable rewards:
kindness, stability, a hardwon acceptance,
a kindling of renewed and renewing warmth.[107]

---

[107] Originally published in Nicola Slee, *The Book of Mary* (SPCK, 2007):
17 (adapted and revised).

Questions for reflection and prayer

- *How do you generally feel when you are returning from holiday or a break away from your work? What do those feelings tell you about yourself and your work? How can they be offered in prayer and into the work itself?*

- *How do you experience your own working environment? Are you aware of having to work in a space and under pressures you would not choose – the haste, waste and noise of which Berry speaks? Is there anything you can do to change and improve this? If not, how do you manage to work within the work environment in ways which are healthy?*

- *Do you recognize the tendency to refuse to rest because your work is never completed? How can you practise daily and nightly laying your work down with a greater degree of trust and thankfulness?*

- *Do you recognize the tendency to think that the well-being of your colleagues and those for whom you care relies wholly on you? Who or what are the 'teachers' who share the work with you and who can help you to recognize that you are not alone?*

- *What might it mean for your work to be 'loving' and 'faithful'?*

Thoughts
and notes